CRIMINAL JUSTICE IN TEXAS TODAY

MICHAEL KANE
Coastal Bend Community College
Beeville, Texas

Prentice Hall

Upper Saddle River, New Jersey 07458

Publisher: Jeff Johnston
Executive Assistant & Supervisor: Brenda Rock
Senior Acquisitions Editor: Kim Davies
Editorial Assistant: Sarah Holle
Managing Editor: Mary Carnis
Production Management: Barbara Cassel
Production Liaison: Adele M. Kupchik
Director of Manufacturing and Production: Bruce Johnson
Manufacturing Buyer: Cathy Petersen
Cover Design: Denise Brown
Cover Design Coordinator: Miguel Ortiz
Interior Design& Formatting: Ellen Cohn
Marketing Manager: Ramona Sherman
Marketing Assistant: Barbara Rosenberg
Marketing Coordinator: Adam Kloza
Printer/Binder: Victor Graphics
Cover Printer: Victor Graphics

Prentice-Hall International (UK) Limited, *London*
Prentice-Hall of Australia Pty. Limited, *Sydney*
Prentice-Hall Canada Inc., *Toronto*
Prentice-Hall Hispanoamericana, S.A., *Mexico*
Prentice-Hall of India Private Limited, *New Delhi*
Prentice-Hall of Japan, Inc., *Tokyo*
Prentice-Hall Singapore Pte. Ltd.
Editora Prentice-Hall do Brasil, Ltda., *Rio de Janeiro*

Prentice Hall

10 9 8 7 6 5 4 3 2 1
ISBN 0-13-089859-7

CONTENTS

PREFACE

Criminal Justice in Texas, a supplement to Frank Schmalleger's ***Criminal Justice Today***, is an introductory look at the practical application of criminal justice in Texas. The supplement will allow students to study the uniqueness and the breadth of the Texas criminal justice system. Students will be exposed to the services of protection and the administration of justice the State of Texas provides to its residents and its visitors.

The supplement showcases the contemporary issues in the Texas criminal justice system. The supplement, reflecting on the timely and thorough research conducted by Frank Schmalleger, used research groups and websites of Texas criminal justice agencies. By utilizing on-line criminal justice databases, the students have the most recent information about the Texas criminal justice system that is possible to print.

The Texas supplement to ***Criminal Justice Today*** is comprehensive and interesting. The supplement addresses all the major elements of the criminal justice system in Texas. Many criminal justice textbooks tend to concentrate on the most prominent areas: police, institutional corrections, and criminal law. The Texas supplement examines crime and the law in Texas, law enforcement throughout the state, the Texas judicial system, corrections in Texas, the juvenile justice system, and the drug problem in Texas.

Last, the supplement encourages student research through the Internet by providing an extensive list of world wide web links to information on criminal justice in Texas. Texas, with its many technology related industries, is a world wide leader in the electronic information age. This leadership has provided an avenue for a vast majority of criminal justice agencies in Texas to publish and maintain their own web page on the Internet.

ACKNOWLEDGMENTS

I am humbly indebted to my wife Carolyn, and my three children, Michael, Alex and Marianne, for their sacrifices which allowed me to complete this supplement. I am very appreciative to all the professionals who shared their criminal justice knowledge and experience. Their generosity in taking time to answer questions about their profession helped this supplement to provide insight to the Texas criminal justice system. I must recognize the following persons for their insight and dedication to their profession:

- Chief Timothy Braaten, Victoria Police Department
- Assistant Warden Charlie Bell, Texas Department of Criminal Justice Institutional Division
- Dr. D. C. "Jim" Dozier, Texas Commission on Law Enforcement Standards and Education

I wish to acknowledge Frank Schmalleger who authored an informative textbook which will enlighten students across the nation.

Lastly, I acknowledge all criminal justice professionals who provide a service which most people are unable to do. These professionals have chosen a career in which service is their reward, and justice is their inspiration. Most of these professionals will never receive the recognition they deserve nor the financial benefits endowed to other professions.

ABOUT THE AUTHOR

Michael Kane, M.A., is a law enforcement/criminal justice instructor and chair of the Protective Services Division at Coastal Bend College, Beeville, Texas. Mr. Kane obtained a bachelor of science degree from the University of Tulsa, majoring in criminal justice. Mr. Kane was awarded a M.A. in Police Administration from Sam Houston State University in 1979. During his studies, Mr. Kane always pursued the concept of police/community satisfaction and, later in his career, customer service. This ideal inspired his masters thesis of "Pre-service and In-service Perception of Police-Community Relations." Today, Michael Kane's work philosophy can best be summarized as "to provide the best possible service combined with a consistent evaluation and quality management process."

Michael Kane participated in an internship with the Tulsa Police Department while enrolled at the University of Tulsa. This internship provided a confirmation of his desire to be part of the criminal justice system. Upon graduation, Mr. Kane was a deputy sheriff with the Harris County Sheriff's Office, serving the unincorporated county surrounding Houston, Texas. Duties at the sheriff's office included being a jailer under the old Texas correctional system using inmate building tenders and hall-men. Mr. Kane was also a patrol officer and later supervisor with Rice University Police Department.

Michael Kane has been employed as an instructor at Coastal Bend College since 1984. Mr. Kane has guided the law enforcement department to grow to the largest on campus, and has also enabled A.A.S. law enforcement graduates to be eligible for testing to be TCLEOSE licensed as Texas peace officers without taking additional academy classes. The customer service concept is apparent by providing college level education and combining it with specific work related skills; this allows graduates immediate access to the criminal justice workforce.

Michael Kane is co-author of ***Action Spanish for Law Enforcement*** (Prentice Hall, 1999). He has directed a police scenario video which accompanies the aforementioned text.

Last, Michael Kane is most proud of the fact he has been married to the same woman, Carolyn, since July 4, 1975. "Carolyn has the ability to make me feel good about myself no matter what events have come to pass."

CHAPTER 1

THE STATE OF TEXAS

INTRODUCTION

Texas is located in the west south central region of the United States. It borders the Gulf of Mexico on the southeast, Mexico on the southwest, New Mexico on the west, Louisiana on the east, and Oklahoma and Arkansas on the north and northeast. The capital city of Texas is Austin. The state motto is "Friendship," the state bird is the mockingbird, the state flower is the bluebonnet, and the state tree is the pecan. Texas' nickname is the "Lone Star State."

THE HISTORY OF TEXAS

Early Texas

Texas was originally inhabited by a variety of Native American tribes, many of which lived in agricultural settlements. Different tribes lived in different regions of Texas. In eastern Texas, the natives were organized into two confederacies, the Hasinai and the Caddo. The Spanish explorers first arriving in eastern Texas met the Hasinai and took their word for allies, "techas," to mean both the area and the people living there. South Texas was home to the Coahuiltecan Indians whereas the Apache lived in the western part of the state.

Spanish Exploration of Texas

The first Europeans to explore Texas were the Spanish, who sent a number of expeditions to the region. Some were explorers; others were searching for gold and other treasures. The first Spanish explorers, led by Alonso Alvarez de Pineda, arrived in Texas in about 1519 while mapping the coast of the Gulf of Mexico. The Spanish also built the first Franciscan missions in Texas in 1682, near what is now El Paso.

The French developed an interest in Texas as well and in 1685, Rene-Robert Cavelier, Sieur de La Salle, established a colony known as Fort Saint Louis. However, the colony was struck by disease and was destroyed by Indians shortly before a Spanish expedition, which also planned to destroy the settlement, arrived. A second attempt at French settlement occurred in 1714, when a French trading expedition founded a settlement on the Rio Grande.

During the late 17th and early 18th centuries, Spain continued to send expeditions into Texas and established missions and forts throughout the region. One of the main reasons for the Spanish development of the mission system in eastern Texas was to prevent further French settlement in what the Spanish considered to be their territory. In 1718, on what is now San Antonio, a fort known as San Antonio de Bexar was built to guard the mission of San Antonio de Valero. The mission was later called the Alamo. San Antonio became the seat of Spanish government in Texas in 1772.

Spanish influence over Texas weakened between 1800 and 1820. In 1821, when Mexico obtained independence from Spain, it claimed Texas as part of the Empire of Mexico. In 1824, Mexico became a republic.

In 1820, Spanish officials in Mexico granted permission for an America, Moses Austin, to establish an American colony in Texas. Austin died soon after. However, after Mexico gained independence from Spain, his son, Stephen F. Austin, was allowed to continue the project. He brought 300 families to Texas, officially establishing a settlement in southeast Texas in 1822. Mexico also gave land grants to other Americans, allowing them to establish colonies in Texas. These contractors were known as ***empresarios*** and they founded a number of colonies during the 1820s. However, friction between Mexico and the American settlers developed: the settlers spoke only English, refused to assimilate into Mexican culture, and advocated slavery, a practice to which the Mexicans were opposed. By 1830, concern about the increasing number of Americans settling in Texas led Mexico to stop American immigration into Texas.

Texas Independence

In 1834, General Antonio Lopez de Santa Anna, a Mexican soldier and politican, became dictator of Mexico, overthrowing the country's constitutional government. This led to the Texas Revolution, in which American colonists began a revolt against Mexico. On December 11, 1835, the colonists captured San Antonio. General Santa Anna marched on the city and attacked the colonists, who retreated into the Alamo. Attacks on the former mission continued until March 6, 1836, when the Alamo fell. During the siege on the Alamo, American Texan rebel leaders declared independence from Mexico and selected Sam Houston as the commander of the rebel army and David Burnet as temporary president. For the next month, Santa Anna forced the rebels to retreat. However, on April 21, 1836, in the Battle of San Jacinto, Sam Houston's army made a surprise attack on the Mexican forces, captured Santa Anna, and ended the war. Santa Anna was forced to recognized Texas' independence and to retreat south of the Rio Grande.

The region became known as the Republic of Texas. The first election was held in September, 1836. Sam Houston was elected president, and the new republic voted to join the United States. However, although the South wanted Texas to become a state, the North was opposed because slavery was allowed in Texas. Texas remained an independent republic for almost ten years.

As more American and European settlers arrived in Texas, Native Americans were forced out of the region. Sam Houston had negotiated a treaty with the Cherokee Indians during the Texas Revolution. The agreement reserved lands in eastern Texas for the Cherokee. However, as Texans had not approved it, the new republic refused to keep the treaty. This led to hostilities between the Cherokee and white settlers. Eventually, the Cherokee were defeated at the Battle of the Neches in 1839 and were forced north to Oklahoma.

Texas in the 19th Century

On December 29, 1845, Texas became the 28th state in the United States. Mexico immediately ended diplomatic relationships with the United States and arguments developed over the location of the Mexico-Texas boundary. In 1846, Congress declared war on Mexico. The Mexican War ended in

1848 with the signing of the Treaty of Guadalupe Hidalgo. Under this treaty, Mexico renounced all claims to Texas and the United States obtained additional land in the southwest that would later become California, Nevada, Utah, and parts of Colorado, Arizona, New Mexico, and Wyoming. The United States also agreed to pay $15 million to Mexico.

During the 1850s Texas was a very attractive destination for settlers, with the northeast region and the area east of Waco and Fort Worth becoming the most popular areas. A total of 89 new counties were organized during this time.

In February 1861, Texas seceded from the United States, despite strong Union feeling in some areas of the state. Governor Sam Houston was removed from office after refusing to take an oath to support the constitution of the Confederate States of America. Texas joined the Confederacy in March and fought for the South during the Civil War. The last battle of the Civil War was fought in Texas, at Palmito Hill, on May 13, 1865; the soldiers had not received the news that General Robert E. Lee had surrendered April 9. Similarly, blacks in Texas did not hear about the 1863 Emancipation Proclamation until June 19, 1865 when the Union Army arrived in Galveston.

During the Reconstructionist period, Texas was dominated by a group known as the Radicals, who sympathized with the North. The Ku Klux Klan rose to power in the state during this period. Texas was readmitted to the Union in 1870 after ratifying the 13th, 14th, and 15th Amendments to the United States Constitution.

The population of Texas increased significantly after the Civil War; between 1870 and 1900 the state moved from the 19th most populous state to the 6th most populous state in the country. Cattle drives became an important part of the Texas economy. By the 1880s, the construction of railroads across the state ended the cattle drives but significantly assisted new settlers in reaching the western portions of the state. Settlers in this region were protected from bandits and hostile Indians by the Texas Rangers, which had been organized in 1835. The railroads also increased the influence of cotton on the state's economy by allowing the crop to be shipped to Houston or St. Louis for international trade. By 1890, the state produced over one-third of all cotton grown in the country.

By the end of the 19th century, Texas was increasingly discriminating against black residents of the state. After the 1896 U.S. Supreme Court case of *Plessey v. Ferguson*, Texas passed "Jim Crow" laws segregating public facilities, residential neighborhoods, and transportation. Black voters were disfranchised, first through violence, then through the development of all-white primaries, and then through the approval of a poll tax. In addition, Mexican residents were also discriminated against and were disfranchised either because they were Mexican citizens or because of the white-only primaries and the poll tax.

Texas During the 20th Century

Texas began to develop oil and gas refineries in 1901. Agriculture also increased as grazing land was irrigated and converted to farmland. Urbanization increased significantly in Texas: the number of cities and towns doubled between 1900 and 1920.

Prior to World War I, a group of Democrats known as Progressives gained control of the party and advocated a number of social and economic reforms (although racial injustice was not one of their concerns). Reforms focused on state institutions, the enfranchisement of white women, and the passage of Prohibition. Progressive Democrats passed laws that created orphanages and state mental institutions. They also reformed the state's prison system, abolishing the convict lease system and segregating prison inmates by sex, race, age, and type of offense.

During World War I, a number of federal military training camps were located in Texas. In 1925, Miriam A. Ferguson was elected the first woman governor of the state, making Texas the second state in the United States (after Wyoming) to have a female governor and the first to have a woman elected to the office. Ferguson's husband, James Ferguson, had previously served as governor of the state as well. Both were staunch opponents of the Ku Klux Klan and helped to reduce its political power in the state.

During World War II, military training camps were again located in Texas, with over 1.25 million troops receiving training in the state. After the war ended, Texas began to move from a rural economy based primarily on farming to an urban industrial economy. In the 1960s, Texas became significantly involved in the United States space program. In 1962, NASA constructed a Manned Spacecraft Center near Houston, which became the headquarters of the manned spacecraft program in 1964. It was renamed the Lyndon B. Johnson Space Center in 1973. The assassination of President John F. Kennedy in Dallas on November 22, 1963, also brought national attention to Texas.

The population of Texas increased significantly during the 1960s; by 1975, Texas had become the third largest state in the country by population. The state's economy focused on oil, defense, and agriculture. By 1970, much of east and west Texas were virtually uninhabited, consisting primarily of enormous farms.

During the 1970s and early 1980s, the state's population and economy were booming. After the 1973 OPEC oil embargo, the price of oil in Texas skyrocketed. However, after the embargo ended in the early 1980s, rapid declines in the prices of natural gas and oil, along with a reduction in the increasingly large amounts spent on defense, greatly damaged the state's economy. The state increased the state sales tax to increase revenue. The state was also under a court order to improve and modernize state prisons; in the early 1990s the governor allocated more funds to improve prisons, as well as roads and bridges. However, this led to a decrease in the monies available for public and higher education. During the 1990s, Texas voters continued to oppose taxes and spending for public services.

Texas' economy began to improve in 1989, leading to renewed immigration into the state. By the early 1990s the state's population increased by 1.5 million. Many Mexicans immigrated to Texas, both legally and illegally, making Hispanics the state's largest minority group.

TEXAS TODAY

Texas is the second largest state in the country by land area; only Alaska has a larger land area. Texas comprises 7 percent of the land area of the United States. The state has a total area of 267,277 square miles, which includes 4,959 square miles of inland water and 404 square miles of coastal water over which the state has jurisdiction. The state runs 770 miles from east to west and 800 miles from north to south. The average elevation of the state is 1,700 feet above sea level.

According to the 1990 census, Texas is the third largest state by population, after California and New York. The 1990 census reported a total population of 17,059,805, an increase of 20 percent over the 1980 figure. The 1998 population estimate was 19,759,614. The average population density is 75 persons per square mile. The most populous city in Texas is Houston, which had a 1996 population of 1,744,058. Other large cities include Dallas, San Antonio, El Paso, Austin, and Fort Worth. In total, Texas has 20 cities with populations of over 100,000.

Approximately 80 percent of the population of Texas lives in urban areas, meaning that they live in or near cities and towns with a population of 2,500 or more. Approximately 90 percent of Texas residents were born in the United States. About 60 percent of those born outside the United States come from Mexico, with Mexican Americans comprising approximately 20 percent of Texas' total population. Other large groups include those of German, Irish, and English descent. In 1990, approximately 75 percent of the state's population was white, 25 percent was Hispanic, and 12 percent was black.

Texas has a total of 254 counties, more than any other state in the United States. The state elects two United States Senators and 30 members of the House of Representatives, for a total of 32 electoral votes. The current state constitution was adopted in 1876.

CRIME STATISTICS IN TEXAS

Schmalleger (see Chapter 2) discusses the development of crime statistics in the United States. The amount of reported crime in Texas rose to a peak in 1991 with over 1,356,000 crimes reported to the police. However, reported crime has continued to decrease since then, with a decline of 20 percent between 1991 and 1998; in 1998 there were 300,00 fewer crimes reported to the police than in 1991. All ***Uniform Crime Reports*** Part I crimes (see Schmalleger, pp. 36-40 and Chapter 3 of this supplement) have decreased with the exception of aggravated assault. Much of the decline in the overall crime rate has resulted from a combination of a significant reduction in property crime in the early 1990s, a decrease in violent crime beginning in 1992, and an increase in the population of the state. In 1988, 8,019 Texans per 100,000 reported some type of crime to the police; in 1998 this number had decreased to 5,110 per 100,000. During this time, the population of Texas increased by approximately 3 million people.

In 1991, the number of violent crimes committed in Texas reached a peak, with over 145,000 violent acts reported to the police. In that year, approximately 839 Texans per 100,000 reported a violent crime to the police; by 1998, this number had declined to 564 per 100,000. The major metropolitan areas of Houston, Dallas-Fort Worth, Austin, El Paso, and San Antonio have all experienced a decline in the rate of violent crime since 1991. Overall, reported murders and robberies in Texas have decreased by approximately 50 percent since 1991.

Property crime peaked in 1988, with 1,236,154 reported crimes, and has declined since; in 1998, less than 900,000 property crimes were reported to the police. Auto theft, a continual problem in Texas with its immense border with Mexico, were reduced by 58 percent between 1988 and 1998. Possibly the most impressive decrease has come in the area of burglary. In 1991, there were approximately 342,000 reported burglaries in Texas; by 1998, that number had declined to approximately 194,000.

Overall, arrests statewide have increased, although there was a slight decrease in 1998. Between 1988 and 1998, the number of arrests for criminal activity increased from approximately 750,000 to over 925,000. Over 10 percent of all arrests are for drug offenses; this percentage is greater than arrests for violent crimes or for Part I property offenses.

State-funded surveys suggest that Texas residents feel safer than they did in the early 1990s. A 1998 survey showed that those surveyed were more likely to be concerned with economy and urban congestion than about crime. Few believe that crime is worse now than in the early 1990s.

CHAPTER 2

INTRODUCTION TO TEXAS CRIMINAL LAW

THE STRUCTURE OF THE GOVERNMENT

Texas law is found in the State Constitution and in the Texas Penal Code. Both have been frequently modified, amended, and altered over the past century.

The current **Texas Constitution** was ratified in 1876. It has been amended numerous times since then. Earlier constitutions were adopted in 1845, 1861, 1866, and 1869. The Texas Constitution is the primary law of the state, although it is subordinate to the United States Constitution. No criminal law or constitutional amendment enacted in Texas may conflict with or violate any individual rights which are guaranteed by the U.S. Constitution, the Bill of Rights, any other Constitutional Amendments, or any federal laws. If any part of the Texas Constitution or legal code is found to be in conflict with the U.S. Constitution or federal statutes, the Texas enactment is unconstitutional and must be changed. See Schmalleger (p.121) for a discussion of the U.S. Constitution.

The procedure for amending the Texas Constitution is discussed in Article 17. The new amendment must be proposed at a regular or special session of the Texas Legislature. The proposed amendment must be approved by a two-thirds majority of the members of each of the two legislative houses. A brief statement explaining the nature of the proposed amendment must be published at least twice in Texas newspapers and must be posed in the courthouse of each county. The proposal must then be approved by a majority of voters before it becomes a part of the state constitution.

Like most states, Texas has three branches of government: executive, legislative, and judicial. This is specified in Article 2 of the Texas Constitution, which also provides for separation of powers.

The Executive Branch

Article 17 of the Texas Constitution discusses Texas' **executive branch**, which consists of the following officers: Governor, Lieutenant Governor, Secretary of State, Comptroller of Public Accounts, Commissioner of the General Land Office, and Attorney General. Most of these officers are elected to four-year terms. Although some states (e.g., California) limit the number of times the governor may be re-elected, in Texas the governor may serve an unlimited number of terms. The other officers, with the exception of the Secretary of State, are also elected by the voters and serve four-year terms as well. The Secretary of State is appointed by the governor with the advice and consent of the Senate.

To be elected to the office of Governor or Lieutenant Governor of Texas, a candidate must be a citizen of the United States, at least 30 years of age, and a state resident for a minimum of five years immediately preceding election to office. The governor has the power to veto legislation that has been proposed by the state legislature. However, a two-thirds vote in both houses of the legislature may override the governor's veto.

George W. Bush III, a Republican, was in his second term as governor when he was elected to the office of President of the United States. Bush resigned on December 21, 2000 and Lieutenant Governor Rick Perry was sworn in as the 47th governor of Texas. Perry will serve as governor for the remainder of Bush's term, which expires in January, 2003.

The Legislative Branch

The **Texas legislature** is discussed in Article III of the Texas Constitution and is the lawmaking branch of the government. The legislature is made up of two houses, a 31-member Senate and a 150-member House of Representatives. All members of the legislature are elected. Senators serve four-year terms whereas representatives serve two-year terms.

To serve as a member of the Texas Senate, a candidate must be a United States citizen, a qualified voter in the state, at least 26 years of age, a state resident for at least five years prior to the election, and a resident of the district from which he/she will be elected for at least one year immediately preceding the election. To serve as a member of the Texas House of Representatives, a candidate must be a United States citizen, a qualified voter, at least 21 years of age, a state resident for at least two years prior to the election, and a resident of the district from which he/she will be elected for at least one year immediately preceding the election.

Each house selects its own officers from among its membership. The presiding officer of the Senate is known as the President Pro Tempore; this officer also performs the duties of the Lieutenant Governor if that office becomes vacant for any reason. The presiding officer of the House of Representatives is known as the Speaker of the House of Representatives.

The Judicial Branch

The judicial branch of the government, which is discussed in Article V of the Texas Constitution, contains the various Texas courts. The court structure of Texas is somewhat more complicated than those of many other states. Texas has a five-level court structure, with two highest-level appellate courts, an intermediate appellate court, state trial courts of general jurisdiction, county trial courts of limited jurisdiction, and local trial courts of limited jurisdiction.

Texas has two top-level appellate courts. The **Texas Supreme Court** has civil jurisdiction while the **Court of Criminal Appeals** has jurisdiction over criminal appeals. The Supreme Court is made up of nine justices, one of whom serves as the chief justice. Justices are elected to six-year terms. To be eligible to serve as a Supreme Court justice, a candidate must be a United States Citizen and a citizen of Texas, must be licenced to practice law in Texas, must be at least 35 years of age, and must have been a practicing lawyer, or a lawyer and judge of a court of record, for at least ten years. The Supreme Court has final appellate jurisdiction in all civil cases and all judicial cases. It generally hears cases which are on appeal from one of the intermediate Courts of Appeals in the state. The Court of Criminal Appeals is composed of nine judges, one of whom serves as the presiding judge. Qualifications to serve as a judge in this court are the same as those required for Supreme Court justices. Judges are elected and serve six-year terms. This court has final appellate jurisdiction over criminal cases. In addition, all cases involving a sentence of death are automatically appealed to the Court of Criminal Appeals from the trial court level.

The state's intermediate appellate courts are known as **Courts of Appeals**. There is one Court of Appeals in each of the fourteen courts of appeals districts. Each Court of Appeals has a Chief Justice and between two and twelve additional justices, all of whom must meet the same qualifications required for Supreme Court justices. These courts have intermediate appellate jurisdiction in criminal and civil cases that have been appealed from district or county courts.

The state is also divided into judicial districts, each of which has a **District Court** with one or more judges. District courts are the state's trial courts of general jurisdiction and have original jurisdiction over all felony criminal cases, as well as civil cases involving at least $200, divorce cases, and various other matters. District judges are elected to four-year terms, must be a citizen of the United States and of Texas, must be licensed to practice law in Texas, must have been a practicing lawyer or judge of a court in Texas for at least four years prior to election, and must have resided in the district from which he/she is elected for at least two years preceding election. District court judges must live in their districts during their terms of office.

Texas has several county-level courts which have limited jurisdiction. Each county has one **Constitutional County Court**, as required by the Texas Constitution. The county judge, the presiding officer of the county court, is elected and serves a four-year term. County courts have limited criminal and civil jurisdiction and in some counties have appellate jurisdiction over cases appealed from justice of the peace or municipal courts. The Constitution specifically limits each county to only one county court. Because of this, larger counties also have **County Courts at Law** to assist the county court. The jurisdiction of county courts at law varies by county. In those counties that have them, the county courts at law (not the county court) have appellate jurisdiction over cases appealed from a justice of the peace or municipal court. Finally, some jurisdictions also have **Statutory Probate Courts** which have original jurisdiction over probate matters, guardianship issues, and mental health commitments. In some counties, specialized probate courts hear only probate matters.

Finally, the state has several local trial courts which also have limited jurisdiction. Each of the approximately 850 incorporated cities and towns in Texas has one or more **Municipal Courts**. Municipal courts have original jurisdiction over violations of city ordinances. In addition, each county in the state is divided into justice of the peace precincts; the number of precincts in a county (between one and eight) is determined by the county population. Each precinct has either one or two **Justice of the Peace Courts**, depending on the precinct population. Justices of the peace are elected to four year terms. Currently, Texas has approximately 900 justice of the peace courts. They have original jurisdiction over minor civil cases as well as certain misdemeanor criminal cases, and also serve as small claims courts.

Passing a Law in Texas

In Texas, a bill may be introduced into either the House or the Senate and, after it has been passed by one of the two legislative houses, it may still be amended by the other. Each bill must first be referred to a committee which reports upon it prior to voting. The bill then goes to a floor vote in the originating house. After it is passed by this house, it is sent to the other house for review, where it may be passed, amended, altered, or rejected. If a bill is considered and defeated by either house, no other bill which contains the same substance may be passed into law during the same legislative session. If the bill passes both houses of the Texas Legislature, it is sent to the governor for approval; he/she may choose either to veto the bill or to sign it into law. The governor has ten days (not counting Sundays) to veto the bill. If the governor approves and signs the bill, or if he/she fails to veto it within ten days, the bill will become law. The legislature may, by a two-thirds vote of each house, enact a bill into law over the governor's veto.

THE TEXAS PENAL CODE

There are several sources of criminal law in Texas (see Schmalleger, pp.119-123, for a discussion of the development of law). These include:

1. Federal and state constitutions
2. Substantive criminal law
3. Case law

Together, the Texas Constitution and the U.S. Constitution provide the basic framework for criminal law, first by focusing on individual rights and on the limitations placed on government power and second by requiring the establishment of a judicial system. However, neither the federal nor the state constitution significantly emphasizes the creation or definition of crimes.

The primary source of **substantive criminal law** in Texas is the **Texas Penal Code**, which is part of the Texas Statutes. Amendments to the state Penal Code must go through the process discussed above (see "Passing a Law in Texas") before becoming a part of the Penal Code. The modern Texas Penal Code was first enacted in 1973. However, other statutes also contain laws which relate to crime and punishment. For example, The Texas Code of Criminal Procedure contains laws relating to procedures such as arrests, trials, and sentencing. Other statutes that define criminal actions include the Family Code, the Transportation Code, the Alcohol Beverage Code, the Agriculture Code, the Business and Commerce Code, the Tax Code, the Education Code, and the Health and Safety Code, among others. See Schmalleger (pp.127-128) for a discussion of criminal law.

Statutory citations from the Texas Penal Code resemble case citations. A sample statutory citation is **Pen §19.01**. Pen is the abbreviation for the Texas Penal Code and 19.01 refers to the specific section number of the statute. This particular statute lists the types of criminal homicide.

The Texas Penal Code was originally based on the English common law (see Schmalleger, pp.120-121), which became the law of the original thirteen colonies and then evolved into the law of the individual states as they entered the union. However, the current Texas legal system is based entirely on written law, so that all crimes are codified. Pen §1.03(a) states that:

> Conduct does not constitute an offense unless it is defined as an offense by statute, municipal ordinance, order of a county commissioners court, or rule authorized by and lawfully adopted under a statute.

Thus, unless a behavior has been specifically defined as an offense, it is not a crime under the law in Texas.

Case law (see Schmalleger, p.133) consists of appellate court decisions or opinions which interpret the meaning of the law. Effectively, case law is made by judges when they hand down decisions in court. Because of the principle of ***stare decisis***, or precedent (see Schmalleger, p.133), a decision made by a judge in one court will be followed by later judges in the state until the same court reverses its decision or until the decision is overturned by a higher court.

The Texas Penal Code contains two types of law, substantive and procedural. Schmalleger (see p.128) defines **substantive criminal law** as "that part of the law that defines crimes and specifies punishments." Chapter 19 of the Penal Code, which defines the various types of criminal homicide, is an example of substantive criminal law. **Procedural law**, on the other hand, is defined by Schmalleger (see p.133) as "the aspect of the law that specifies the methods to be used in enforcing substantive law." In other words, procedural law outlines the rules that the state must follow when dealing with crimes and criminals. These include the procedures that must be used to investigate crimes, arrest suspects, and carry out formal prosecution. The protection against double jeopardy is an example of procedural law.

THE DEFINITION AND CLASSIFICATION OF CRIME

Schmalleger (see pp.122-123) discusses the distinction between *mala in se* and *mala prohibita* crimes. These terms, which date back to the common law, relate to the seriousness of an offense. ***Mala in se*** crimes involve behaviors that are considered to be inherently wrong or evil in and of themselves. Murder, rape, arson, and incest are examples of *mala in se* crimes. ***Mala prohibita*** crimes are behaviors that are wrong only because they have been forbidden by legislative act, not because they are considered to be inherently evil. Examples of *mala prohibita* crimes include traffic violations and drug use. However, these terms are not found in the Texas Penal Code.

Schmalleger (see pp.134-136) discusses the varies types or categories of violations of the criminal law. According to Pen §12.02, "offenses are designated as felonies or misdemeanors." In Texas, the difference between the two types of crimes is not determined by the offense itself, or by the action committed by the offender, but by the possible punishment or by the designation of the crime as a felony or a misdemeanor by the Penal Code.

Felonies (see Schmalleger, p.134) are the most serious offenses in Texas. Pen §107(a)(23) defines a felony as "an offense so designated by law or punishable by death or confinement in a penitentiary." A **misdemeanor** is defined in Pen §107(a)(31) as "an offense so designated by law or punishable by fine, by confinement in jail, or by both fine and confinement in jail." Thus, even if the Penal Code does not specifically identify a crime as a misdemeanor or a felony, the classification can easily be inferred from the prescribed sentence.

Felonies are classified into five categories, based on the relative seriousness of the crime. The five categories are listed in Pen §12.04 and the associated punishments are outlined in Pen §12.31 through Pen §12.35. The most serious category is a **capital felony**, which is punishable either by death or by life imprisonment in a state prison. A **felony of the first degree** is punishable by imprisonment in a state prison for life, or by a term of imprisonment for not more than 99 years or for less than five years. The key difference between a life sentence and a sentence of 99 years is that a life sentence may not be discharged. A **felony of the second degree** is punishable by a term of imprisonment in a state prison for not more than 20 years or less than two years. A **felony of the third degree** is punishable by imprisonment in a state prison for a term of not more than ten years nor less than two years. Finally, a **state jail felony** is punishable by confinement in a state jail facility for a term of not more than two years nor less than 180 days. In addition to the terms of imprisonment mandated for the above felony categories, the offender may be required to pay a fine of not more than $10,000; the fine is in addition to (not in lieu of) incarceration.

Misdemeanors (see Schmalleger, p.134) are also classified by degree; according to Pen §12.03(a), a misdemeanor may be a Class A, Class B, or Class C misdemeanor. If a statute defining a crime as a misdemeanor does not specify the degree, it is considered to be a Class C misdemeanor. The penalties associated with misdemeanors are outlined in Pen §12.21 through Pen §12.23. A **Class A misdemeanor** is punishable by either a fine of up to $4,000 or a term of imprisonment in a jail for no more than one year, or both the fine and term of imprisonment. A **Class B misdemeanor** is punishable by either a fine of no more than $2,000 or a jail term of no more than 180 days, or both. Finally, a **Class C misdemeanor** is punishable by a fine of no more than $500.

Schmalleger (see pp.135-136) also discusses the concept of **inchoate offenses**. He defines an inchoate offense as: "An offense not yet completed. Also, an offense that consists of an action or conduct that is a step toward the intended commission of another offense." Inchoate offenses recognized in Texas include **criminal attempt** (Pen §15.01), **criminal conspiracy** (Pen §15.02), and **criminal solicitation** (Pen §15.03 and Pen §15.031).

The Criminal Act (*Actus Reus*) and Intent (*Mens Rea*)

Schmalleger (see pp.136-140) discusses the general features of a crime. One element is ***actus reus***, or the **criminal act** (see Schmalleger, p.136). According to Pen §6.01,

> (a) A person commits an offense only if he voluntarily engages in conduct, including an act, an omission, or possession.
>
> (b) Possession is a voluntary act if the possessor knowingly obtains or receives the thing possessed or is aware of his control of the thing for a sufficient time to permit him to terminate his control.
>
> (c) A person who omits to perform an act does not commit an offense unless a law as defined by Section 1.07 provides that the omission is an offense or otherwise provides that he has a duty to perform the act.

Most criminal acts are deliberate and voluntary on the part of the offender. However, the act necessary to make up a crime will vary with each crime. Verbal actions (words) can be a sufficient action in, for example, the crime of perjury. Merely possessing something may be a sufficient act if the crime is one that involves illegal possession of goods (for example, possession of illegal drugs).

It is clear from Pen §6.01 that the criminal act may also consist of some form of omission or failure to act. An **omission** occurs when someone who has a legal duty to act fails to perform an action that is required by law. For example, a security guard who deliberately looks the other way while company property is stolen is a passive participant and is guilty of omission to act. Similarly, a parent or other legal caretaker who fails to adequately feed and shelter an infant, resulting in the death of the child, has committed a crime by his or her failure to act.

Failing to act is only a crime of omission when an individual has a legal duty to act in that situation. For example, consider the case of a swimmer at a local public pool who develops a cramp while in deep water. The lifeguard on duty at the pool has a legal duty to act and, if he/she fails to go to the swimmer's assistance, would be guilty of a crime of omission. However, the other swimmers in the pool have only a moral duty to aid the distressed swimmer and if they fail to provide assistance would not be guilty of any crime. In addition, the omission or failure to act must also be voluntary for this statute to apply.

In addition to the act or omission, Schmalleger (see p.137) discusses the element of ***mens rea***, or the **guilty mind**. Pen §6.02 states that:

> (a) Except as provided in Subsection (b), a person does not commit an offense unless he intentionally, knowingly, recklessly, or with criminal negligence engages in conduct as the definition of the offense requires.
>
> (b) If the definition of an offense does not prescribe a culpable mental state, a culpable mental state is nevertheless required unless the definition plainly dispenses with any mental element.
>
> (c) If the definition of an offense does not prescribe a culpable mental state, but one is nevertheless required under Subsection (b), intent, knowledge, or recklessness suffices to establish criminal responsibility.
>
> (d) Culpable mental states are classified according to relative degrees, from highest to lowest, as follows:
> (1) intentional;
> (2) knowing;
> (3) reckless;
> (4) criminal negligence.
>
> (e) Proof of a higher degree of culpability than that charged constitutes proof of the culpability charged.

Thus, some form of **culpable mental state** is required for a crime to occur. Culpable mental states are specifically defined in Pen §6.03. A crime is committed **intentionally** when the offender consciously desires to engage in the conduct or cause the outcome. The offender does not have to declare intent to be convicted of a crime; the intent may be inferred by the actions of the offender. A crime is committed **knowingly** when the offender is aware that his/her conduct violates the law and/or is aware that his/her conduct will cause a certain result. An crime is committed **recklessly** when the offender is aware of the risk of his/her actions and consciously disregards that risk. The risk must be substantial and unjustified and disregarding it must be a significant deviation from the behavior of a reasonable person. Finally, a crime is committed with **criminal negligence** when the offender fails to perceive a risk that would be perceived by any reasonable person. The key difference between recklessness and criminal negligence is that, to be negligent, the offender does not have to consciously be aware of the risk involved by his/her behavior.

DEFENSES TO A CRIMINAL CHARGE

Schmalleger (pp.143-160) discusses in detail the topic of defenses to a criminal charge, outlining several specific categories of defenses. Many of these defenses are specifically mentioned in the Florida Statutes or the Florida Rules of Criminal Procedure.

Justifications

Schmalleger (p.143) defines **justifications** as "a legal defense in which the defendant admits committing the act in question but claims it was necessary to avoid some greater evil." Justifications that exclude criminal responsibility are discussed in Chapter 9 of the Texas Penal Code. Probably the most well-known justification defense is that of **self-defense** (see Schmalleger, p.144), in which the defendant claims that the use of force against the victim was justifiable because it was the only way the defendant could ensure his/her own safety. Pen 9.31 states that

> (a) Except as provided in Subsection (b), a person is justified in using force against another when and to the degree he reasonably believes the force is immediately necessary to protect himself against the other's use or attempted use of unlawful force.
>
> (b) The use of force against another is not justified:
> - (1) in response to verbal provocation alone;
> - (2) to resist an arrest or search that the actor knows is being made by a peace officer, or by a person acting in a peace officer's presence and at his direction, even though the arrest or search is unlawful, unless the resistance is justified under Subsection (c);
> - (3) if the actor consented to the exact force used or attempted by the other;
> - (4) if the actor provoked the other's use or attempted use of unlawful force, unless:
>   - (A) the actor abandons the encounter, or clearly communicates to the other his intent to do so reasonably believing he cannot safely abandon the encounter; and
>   - (B) the other nevertheless continues or attempts to use unlawful force against the actor; or
> - (5) if the actor sought an explanation from or discussion with the other person concerning the actor's differences with the other person while the actor was:
>   - (A) carrying a weapon in violation of Section 46.02; or
>   - (B) possessing or transporting a weapon in violation of Section 46.05.
>
> (c) The use of force to resist an arrest or search is justified:

(1) if, before the actor offers any resistance, the peace officer (or person acting at his direction) uses or attempts to use greater force than necessary to make the arrest or search; and
(2) when and to the degree the actor reasonably believes the force is immediately necessary to protect himself against the peace officer's (or other person's) use or attempted use of greater force than necessary.

(d) The use of deadly force is not justified under this subchapter except as provided in Sections 9.32, 9.33, and 9.34.

Deadly force is defined by Pen §9.01(3) as:

> force that is intended or known by the actor to cause, or in the manner of its use or intended use is capable of causing, death or serious bodily injury.

Deadly force may only be used in the defense of one's self (Pen §9.32), in the defense of a third person (Pen §9.33), or in an emergency situation to protect the life of the person against which the force is being used (Pen §9.34).

Schmalleger (p.145) also discusses the issue of **defense of home and property**. Pen §9.41 makes it clear that force may be used to protect property if the defendant reasonably believed that the force used was necessary at that immediate moment to prevent or stop trespass or illegal interference with property. Force may only be used to recover property if it is used immediately or in fresh pursuit of after the property was taken. Deadly force may only be used to protect property under very limited circumstances, according to Pen §9.42.

Another justification defense discussed in Schmalleger is that of **consent** (see p.146). This defense claims that the injured person consented to the actions that caused the injury. Consent is defined in Pen §1.07(11) as "assent in fact, whether express or apparent." This defense seems to be most commonly used in sex-related offenses, such as sexual assault. For example, in Pen §22.011, the definition of sexual assault specifically states that the actions must be committed without the consent of the other person. The statute makes it clear that coerced consent, obtained through threats of force or violence against the victim or another person, does not constitute a defense of consent.

Excuses

Schmalleger (p.143) defines an **excuse** as:

> a legal defense in which the defendant claims that some personal condition or circumstance at the time of the act was such that he or she should not be held accountable under the criminal law.

The category of excuses is discussed in Schmalleger on pp.146-152. One defense that falls into this category is that of **duress** (see Schmalleger, p.146). This defense is defined in Pen §8.05 and is applied differently to felony and misdemeanor offenses. For the defense of duress to a felony, the defendant must show that he/she committed the crime while under some type of threat of imminent death or serious bodily harm to him/herself or a third person. For the defense of duress to a misdemeanor, the defendant is required only to show that he/she was compelled to commit the crime by force or threat of force (the requirement of imminency does not apply).

The defense of **age** or **infancy** (see Schmalleger, pp.146-147) also falls into this category. According to Pen §8.07, individuals may not be prosecuted for or convicted of crimes committed when they were under the age of 15, with the exceptions of perjury, traffic offenses, and certain Class C misdemeanors (e.g., truancy). In addition, the death penalty may not be imposed on any individual for a crime committed when he/she was less than 17 years of age. There have been some recent unsuccessful legislative attempts in Texas to lower this limit to 16 years of age.

Schmalleger (see p.147) discusses the defense of **mistake**, including both **mistake of law** and **mistake of fact**. While in most cases, the old saying that "ignorance of the law is no defense" is true, there are some exceptions. Pen §8.02(a) states that,

> It is a defense to prosecution that the actor through mistake formed a reasonable belief about a matter of fact if his mistaken belief negated the kind of culpability required for commission of the offense.

Effectively, criminal intent may be negated if the defendant developed a reasonable but erroneous belief that eliminated the intent. This may not be used as a defense in criminal negligence cases. In addition, Pen §8.03(b) states that,

> (b) It is an affirmative defense to prosecution that the actor reasonably believed the conduct charged did not constitute a crime and that he acted in reasonable reliance upon:
> (1) an official statement of the law contained in a written order or grant of permission by an administrative agency charged by law with responsibility for interpreting the law in question; or
> (2) a written interpretation of the law contained in an opinion of a court of record or made by a public official charged by law with responsibility for interpreting the law in question.

Thus, simple ignorance of the law in and of itself still is not a defense. However, defendants who mistakenly thought that they did know the law, and who based this belief on official statements by the government or a public official, may be able to use mistake of law as a defense.

Probably the most well-known (and controversial) defense in this category is that of **insanity** (see Schmalleger, pp.148-152). Although the term insanity is no longer used by mental health professionals, it is a legal term referring to a defense that is based on the defendant's claim that he/she was mentally ill or mentally incapacitated at the time of the offense.

In Texas, insanity is discussed in Pen §8.01. The statute states that,

> (a) It is an affirmative defense to prosecution that, at the time of the conduct charged, the actor, as a result of severe mental disease or defect, did not know that his conduct was wrong.

It is clear from this section of the statute that Texas uses the **M'Naghten Rule** as a test for insanity (see Schmalleger, pp.148-149).

For the defense of insanity to be used, the defense must give notice of their intent to present evidence on insanity at least ten days prior to trial. The burden of proof is on the defendant to prove that he/she did not know that his/her conduct was wrong, because of a severe mental disease or defect. If the defendant is acquitted of criminal charges using the insanity defense, he/she will be found **not guilty by reason of insanity**. However, even though the defendant has been acquitted of the charges, he/she may not be set free but may be committed for as long as he/she remains mentally ill.

Procedural Defenses

Schmalleger (see p.143) defines a **procedural defense** as:

> A defense which claims that the defendant was in some significant way discriminated against in the justice process or that some important aspect of official procedure was not properly followed in the investigation or prosecution of the crime charged.

Schmalleger discusses the topic of procedural defenses on pp.152-155. Effectively, these defenses claim that some form of procedural law was not properly followed. One of the defenses covered in Schmalleger (see pp.152-153) is **entrapment**. Pen §8.06(a) discusses the issue of entrapment, stating that,

> It is a defense to prosecution that the actor engaged in the conduct charged because he was induced to do so by a law enforcement agent using persuasion or other means likely to cause persons to commit the offense. Conduct merely affording a person an opportunity to commit an offense does not constitute entrapment.

The entrapment defense, which is extremely difficult for the defendant to prove, is most commonly used when the defendant was caught in an undercover police action; one of the the most frequent uses seems to relate to the sale of illegal drugs. In general, the defendant will claim that he/she does not regularly sell drugs but made a sale as a favor to the undercover officer. One of the most common ways for the police to prevent the use of this defense is to make two or more purchases from the same suspect; after the suspect has made multiple sales, the jury is more likely to believe that the undercover officer simply provided the defendant with an opportunity to commit the crime, rather than that the officer induced or encouraged the defendant to engage in a behavior in which he/she would not normally become involved.

Another defense is that of the **denial of a speedy trial** (see Schmalleger, p.155). In Texas, the right to a speedy trial is guaranteed in Article I, Section 10, of the Texas Constitution as well as in Article 1.05 of the Code of Criminal Procedure (CCrP). The time limit for a trial to be "speedy" is, in most cases, 60 to 180 days, depending on the seriousness of the offense. This time limit may be extended under certain circumstances. Obviously, if the defendant has requested an extension, he/she may not later claim that his/her right to a speedy trial was denied. However, if the time limit has not been extended by request and if there are no exceptional circumstances which caused a delay, the court must discharge the defendant from custody.

Another issue is that of **double jeopardy** (see Schmalleger, pp.153-154). Article I, Section 14, of the Texas Constitution states that,

> No person, for the same offense, shall be twice put in jeopardy of life or liberty, nor shall a person be again put upon trial for the same offense, after a verdict of not guilty in a court of competent jurisdiction.

This statement is repeated in CCrP 1.10. In addition, CCrP 1.11 states that,

> An acquittal of the defendant exempts him from a second trial or a second prosecution for the same offense, however irregular the proceedings may have been; but if the defendant shall have been acquitted upon trial in a court having no jurisdiction of the offense, he may be prosecuted again in a court having jurisdiction.

Innovative Defenses

Finally, Schmalleger (see pp.156-160) discusses the topic of **innovative defenses**, which are all relatively new and novel defenses against conviction. However, these defenses are not specifically discussed in the Texas Penal Code.

CHAPTER 3

INDEX CRIMES

INTRODUCTION

The Federal Bureau of Investigation annually publishes the ***Uniform Crime Reports*** (UCR), the most widely used source of official data on crime and criminals in the United States. Schmalleger (see pp.33-53) discusses the UCR in detail. Much of the UCR deals with **index crimes**, a set of eight serious offenses that the FBI uses as a measure of crime in the United States. They are also known as **Part I Offenses**. Four of them are violent crimes; the other four are property crimes. The eight index crimes measured by the FBI are:

- homicide
- forcible rape
- robbery
- aggravated assault
- burglary
- larceny-theft
- motor vehicle theft
- arson

However, the definitions used by the FBI in compiling the UCR are not always the same as those found in the Texas Penal Code. This chapter will discuss the definitions of these eight serious crimes as provided by Texas state statutes.

All crimes defined in the Penal Code of Texas are classified by the seriousness of the crime. For example, manslaughter is a second degree felony. Chapter 12 of the Texas Penal Code discusses ordinary and exceptional punishments for each class of offense. These will be discussed in detail in the chapter on sentencing.

CRIMINAL HOMICIDE

Homicide is the killing of one human being by another. If that killing is illegal, then it is a form of **criminal homicide**. Schmalleger discusses the crime of criminal homicide, or murder, on pp.40-41 and on pp.140-142. Texas' criminal homicide statute is found in Chapter 19 of the Penal Code. According to Pen §19.01:

> (a) A person commits criminal homicide if he intentionally, knowingly, recklessly, or with criminal negligence causes the death of an individual.
>
> (b) Criminal homicide is murder, capital murder, manslaughter, or criminally negligent homicide.

Other deaths are not considered homicides in Texas.

All the homicide offenses are discussed in the Texas Penal Code contain two key elements:

- conduct that causes the death of an individual, and
- the mental culpability of the defendant

Effectively, these elements are the guilty act (*actus reus*) and the guilty mind (*mens rea*).

The specific homicide offense of which a defendant may be convicted depends on his/her level of mental culpability and on the nature of the circumstances surrounding the death (e.g., the presence of aggravating factors).

As stated in Pen §19.02, Texas recognizes four specific types of criminal homicide:

- murder (defined in Pen §19.02)
- capital murder (defined in Pen §19.03)
- manslaughter (defined in Pen §19.04)
- criminal negligent homicide (defined in Pen §19.05)

The state also recognizes felony murder as the only form of murder which does not require a direct relationship between the defendant's murderous conduct and his/her the mental state. No intent to commit murder is required for a conviction of felony murder.

Murder

Pen §19.02 discusses the crime of murder (see Schmalleger, pp.140-141), stating that:

> (b) A person commits an offense if he:
> (1) intentionally or knowingly causes the death of an individual;
> (2) intends to cause serious bodily injury and commits an act clearly dangerous to human life that causes the death of an individual; or
> (3) commits or attempts to commit a felony, other than manslaughter, and in the course of and in furtherance of the commission or attempt, or in immediate flight from the commission or attempt, he commits or attempts to commit an act clearly dangerous to human life that causes the death of an individual.

Unless the defense can prove that the crime was committed under the influence of a sudden passion, murder is a first degree felony.

Essentially, this statute defines three different types of first degree murder.

1. **Intentional or knowing murder** - the offender who caused the death of another person had the specific and conscious intent to do so.

2. **Transferred intent murder** - the offender intended to cause serious bodily injury to another person and, while voluntarily committing a dangerous act, actually caused the death of the other person. Because the offender does not have to have the intent to kill, only to cause serious bodily harm, this is a form of transferred intent.

3. **Felony murder** - the offender consciously intended to commit a felony (other than manslaughter) and, during the commission of the felony, caused the death of another person. The intent to commit the murder is taken from the intent to commit the felony.

The statute also defines one type of second degree murder, the **crime of passion**. Essentially, if the offender is found guilty of first degree murder and can then show, at the punishment stage of the trial, that the crime was committed in the heat of passion, the crime is essentially reduced to voluntary manslaughter and punished as a second degree felony.

First degree murder is punishable by imprisonment in a state prison for life or for a term of not less than five years nor more than 99 years.

Capital Murder

The general murder statute defines murder as a first degree felony. First degree felonies are not punishable by death. However, under some circumstances, criminal homicide becomes a capital felony, which is punishable either by life imprisonment or by a sentence of death. Capital murder includes two key elements:

1. The offender intentionally or knowingly causes the death of another person (murder), and

2. At least one of eight additional aggravating factors is present.

According to Pen §19.03(a), the aggravating factors that elevate first degree murder to capital murder are:

(1) the person murders a peace officer or fireman who is acting in the lawful discharge of an official duty and who the person knows is a peace officer or fireman;
(2) the person intentionally commits the murder in the course of committing or attempting to commit kidnapping, burglary, robbery, aggravated sexual assault, arson, or obstruction or retaliation;
(3) the person commits the murder for remuneration or the promise of remuneration or employs another to commit the murder for remuneration or the promise of remuneration;
(4) the person commits the murder while escaping or attempting to escape from a penal institution;
(5) the person, while incarcerated in a penal institution, murders another:
(A) who is employed in the operation of the penal institution; or

    (B) with the intent to establish, maintain, or participate in a combination or in the profits of a combination;
(6) the person:
    (A) while incarcerated for an offense under this section or Section 19.02, murders another; or
    (B) while serving a sentence of life imprisonment or a term of 99 years for an offense under Section 20.04, 22.021, or 29.03, murders another;
(7) the person murders more than one person:
    (A) during the same criminal transaction; or
    (B) during different criminal transactions but the murders are committed pursuant to the same scheme or course of conduct; or
(8) the person murders an individual under six years of age.

If none of these aggravating factors are present, the offender may still be convicted of murder or some other lesser offense. However, the offender may not be sentenced to the death penalty. Capital murder is the only death penalty offense that has ever existed in Texas.

Manslaughter

According to Pen §19.04, manslaughter occurs when the offender "recklessly causes the death of an individual." Essentially, the offender is involved in an action, knows that there is a substantial and unjustifiable risk of death to another person as a result of this action, and consciously disregards that risk in a situation when a reasonable person would not disregard it. Actual intent to kill is not a required element of this crime. In fact, there is no such thing as the crime of attempted manslaughter in Texas because by definition an attempt requires the presence of intent. See Schmalleger (p.141) for a discussion of manslaughter.

Manslaughter is a second degree felony in Texas, calling for a term of incarceration in a state prison for a term of not less than two nor more than twenty years.

Criminally Negligent Homicide

Criminally negligent homicide (see Schmalleger, p.141) is the lowest level or category of homicide in Texas. According to Pen §19.05, an offender commits the crime of criminally negligent homicide "if he causes the death of an individual by criminal negligence." They key difference between criminally negligent homicide and manslaughter is the type of culpable mental state required as an element of the crime. Both involve a lack of deliberate intent to kill. However, manslaughter involves a crime that is committed recklessly; criminally negligent homicide involves a crime that is only committed with criminal negligence. Pen §6.03(d) defines criminal negligence, stating that:

> A person acts with criminal negligence, or is criminally negligent, with respect to circumstances surrounding his conduct or the result of his conduct when he ought to be aware of a substantial and unjustifiable risk that the circumstances exist or the result will occur. The risk must be of such a nature and degree that the failure to perceive it constitutes a gross deviation from the standard of care that an ordinary person would exercise under all the circumstances as viewed from the actor's standpoint.

Essentially, the offender does not perceive a risk that any reasonable person would perceive. As with manslaughter, there is no attempted negligent homicide as the crime by definition does not involve an intent to kill.

In Texas, criminally negligent homicide is frequently used in cases of fatal motor vehicle accidents that do not involve drugs or alcohol but that do involve one or more aggravating negligent factors, such as speeding or tailgating during rush hour. The crime is a state jail felony, which is punishable by incarceration in a state jail facility for a term of not less than 180 days or more than two years.

FORCIBLE RAPE

Schmalleger discusses the crime of **forcible rape** on pp.42-45. In the Uniform Crime Reporting Program, forcible rape is defined as "the carnal knowledge of a female forcibly and against her will." This originally reflected the prevailing definitions used in many states in the United States. However, during the 1980s and 1990s, the Texas Penal Code relating to sexual offenses was significantly revised. The crimes of "rape," "sexual abuse," and "rape of a child/statutory rape" were reclassified from sexual offenses to assaultive offenses. In addition, the marital exemption clause, which excluded spouses as victims of sexual assaults, was eliminated. Therefore, men who rape or sexually abuse their wives may no longer use their marital state as a defense. See Schmalleger (p.42) for a discussion of women sexually assaulted by husbands, boyfriends, and dates, and Schmalleger (p.45) for a discussion of rape within marriage.

Currently, there are two main types of "rape" in Texas:

- sexual assault
- aggravated sexual assault

The Penal Law still includes a chapter entitled "Sexual Offenses" (Chapter 21 of the Texas Penal Law), but this now includes crimes such as public lewdness, indecency with a child, and homosexual conduct. Assaultive crimes, including crimes of sexual assault, are discussed in Chapter 22 of the Texas Penal Law.

Sexual assault is defined in Pen §22.011(a). The statute states that:

> A person commits an offense if the person:
> (1) intentionally or knowingly:
> (A) causes the penetration of the anus or female sexual organ of another person by any means, without that person's consent;
> (B) causes the penetration of the mouth of another person by the sexual organ of the actor, without that person's consent; or
> (C) causes the sexual organ of another person, without that person's consent, to contact or penetrate the mouth, anus, or sexual organ of another person, including the actor; or
> (2) intentionally or knowingly:
> (A) causes the penetration of the anus or female sexual organ of a child by any means;

(B) causes the penetration of the mouth of a child by the sexual organ of the actor;
(C) causes the sexual organ of a child to contact or penetrate the mouth, anus, or sexual organ of another person, including the actor;
(D) causes the anus of a child to contact the mouth, anus, or sexual organ of another person, including the actor; or
(E) causes the mouth of a child to contact the anus or sexual organ of another person, including the actor.

This statute includes two specific types of behavior. The first [outlined in Pen §22.011(a)(1)] involves non-consensual intercourse of various types between adults, regardless of their marital status. The second [outlined in Pen §22.011(a)(2)] involves any intercourse, regardless of the consensual or non-consensual nature, between an adult and a child. A child is defined by Pen §22.011(c)(1) as an individual who is less than 17 years of age and who is not the spouse of the actor. Thus, sexual relations involving spouses, when one or both are below the age of 17, do not fall under this statute.

Most elements of this statute are gender-neutral and do not indicate the gender of the victim or the offender. However, Sections (1)(a) and(2)(a) of the statute specifically indicate a female victim, although they do not specify the gender of the assailant.

The most commonly used defenses to sexual assault of an adult victim are consent and lack of penetration. Consent is not a defense against intercourse with a child. However, Pen §22.011(e) states that if the offender is no more than three years older than the victim and the victim is at least 14 years of age, the defendant has an affirmative defense against the crime.

Sexual assault is a second degree felony.

Aggravated sexual assault is defined in Pen §22.021(a). The statute states that:

A person commits an offense:
(1) if the person:
(A) intentionally or knowingly:
(i) causes the penetration of the anus or female sexual organ of another person by any means, without that person's consent;
(ii) causes the penetration of the mouth of another person by the sexual organ of the actor, without that person's consent; or
(iii) causes the sexual organ of another person, without that person's consent, to contact or penetrate the mouth, anus, or sexual organ of another person, including the actor; or
(B) intentionally or knowingly:
(i) causes the penetration of the anus or female sexual organ of a child by any means;

(ii) causes the penetration of the mouth of a child by the sexual organ of the actor;
(iii) causes the sexual organ of a child to contact or penetrate the mouth, anus, or sexual organ of another person, including the actor;
(iv) causes the anus of a child to contact the mouth, anus, or sexual organ of another person, including the actor; or
(v) causes the mouth of a child to contact the anus or sexual organ of another person, including the actor; and

(2) if:
(A) the person:
(i) causes serious bodily injury or attempts to cause the death of the victim or another person in the course of the same criminal episode;
(ii) by acts or words places the victim in fear that death, serious bodily injury, or kidnapping will be imminently inflicted on any person;
(iii) by acts or words occurring in the presence of the victim threatens to cause the death, serious bodily injury, or kidnapping of any person;
(iv) uses or exhibits a deadly weapon in the course of the same criminal episode; or
(v) acts in concert with another who engages in conduct described by Subdivision (1) directed toward the same victim and occurring during the course of the same criminal episode;
(vi) administers or provides flunitrazepam, otherwise known as rohypnol, or gamma hydroxbutyrate to the victim of the offense with the intent of facilitating the commission of the offense;
(B) the victim is younger than 14 years of age; or
(C) the victim is 65 years of age or older.

The first part of this statute [Pen §22.021(a)(1)] is virtually identical to the sexual assault statute outlined above. The second part of this statute [Pen §22.021(a)(2)] lists a number of aggravating factors which increase the seriousness of the crime. The first group of aggravating factors relate to the behavior of the offender. These include causing serious bodily injury to the victim, placing the victim in fear of death or serious bodily injury, placing the victim in fear of death or serious bodily injury to a third person, using or showing a deadly weapon, gang rape, and the use of "date rape" drugs such as rohypnol or GHB. The second group of aggravating factors involves the age of the victim: the crime is elevated from sexual assault to aggravated sexual assault if the victim is less than 14 or more than 64 years of age.

Aggravated sexual assault is a first degree felony.

ROBBERY

Schmalleger discusses the crime of **robbery** on p. 45. Texas recognizes two categories of this crime: robbery and aggravated robbery. Pen §29.02(a) defines robbery as:

> A person commits an offense if, in the course of committing theft as defined in Chapter 31 and with intent to obtain or maintain control of the property, he:
> (1) intentionally, knowingly, or recklessly causes bodily injury to another; or
> (2) intentionally or knowingly threatens or places another in fear of imminent bodily injury or death.

The term "in the course of committing theft" includes any behavior that occurs during an attempt to commit a theft, during the actual commission of a theft, or during the immediate flight from the theft or attempted theft. Property is defined in Pen §29.01(2) as including:

> (A) tangible or intangible personal property including anything severed from land; or
> (B) a document, including money, that represents or embodies anything of value.

Thus, in Texas, robbery basically involves some type of assaultive behavior that occurs:

1. during the commission of a theft
2. during an attempted theft
3. during the offender's immediate flight after committing or attempting to commit a theft.

Essentially, robbery is a combination of assault and theft; a crime that involves the use of force or fear to illegally obtain the personal property of another person. The key difference between robbery and theft is the presence of the assaultive conduct; the key difference between robbery and assault is the attempt to acquire the property of another. For the crime of robbery to be proved, some connection must be shown between the assaultive behavior and the theft, so that the assault was committed specifically for the purpose of committing the theft or escaping after the theft.

Some states (e.g., New York) require an actual theft or larceny as an element of the crime of robbery. However, in Texas, even if no property is actually taken, the defendant may be found guilty of the crime of robbery if it can be shown that he/she attempted to take the property of another. Thus, specific intent to obtain the property of another, even if the property was not actually obtained, is sufficient.

The use of force or the threat of force is also a required element of robbery. In addition, the offender must have intended the assaultive conduct. In the case of actual bodily harm, the level of intent may be intentional, knowingly, or recklessly. In the case of threat or fear, the level of intent may be intentionally or knowingly (but not recklessly). The threat does not need to be verbal; threats implied by the offender's conduct are sufficient to meet the statutory requirement.

Aggravated robbery is essentially the crime of robbery as defined in Pen §29.02 with one or more specifically identified aggravating factors present. The crime is defined in Pen §29.03(a), which states that:

> A person commits an offense if he commits robbery as defined in Section 29.02, and he:
> (1) causes serious bodily injury to another;
> (2) uses or exhibits a deadly weapon; or
> (3) causes bodily injury to another person or threatens or places another person in fear of imminent bodily injury or death, if the other person is:
> (A) 65 years of age or older; or
> (B) a disabled person.

The first two aggravating factors involve behaviors of the offender: causing serious bodily injury to the victim while committing the robbery, or using or displaying a deadly weapon in the course of the robbery. The third factor focuses on the status of the victim; the crime is considered more serious if the victim is disabled or over the age of 64.

Aggravated robbery is a first degree felony.

AGGRAVATED ASSAULT

There is often some confusion about the actual meaning of **assault**. In many states, assault does not involve the infliction of any injury upon another person, it is merely the intentional attempt or threat to cause injury. In these states, when an injury is actually inflicted, a **battery** has occurred. The Uniform Crime Reporting Program defines aggravated assault as:

> an unlawful attack by one person upon another for the purpose of inflicting severe or aggravated bodily injury. This type of assault is usually accompanied by the use of a weapon or by means likely to produce death or great bodily harm.

In Texas, however, one of the possible elements of assault is the infliction of some type of bodily injury to another person. Thus, there is no crime of battery in Texas.

The crime of assault is discussed in Chapter 22 of the Texas Penal Code, which includes both assault and aggravated assault. As with other crimes, the more serious offense includes all the elements of the lesser offense with the addition of one or more aggravating factors. Schmalleger discusses the crimes of simple and aggravated assault on p.48.

Pen §22.02(a) defines the crime of **assault**, stating that:

> A person commits an offense if the person:
> (1) intentionally, knowingly, or recklessly causes bodily injury to another, including the person's spouse;

(2) intentionally or knowingly threatens another with imminent bodily injury, including the person's spouse; or
(3) intentionally or knowingly causes physical contact with another when the person knows or should reasonably believe that the other will regard the contact as offensive or provocative.

Thus, this statute essentially includes three specific types of behavior:

1. Actually causing bodily injury to a victim
2. Threatening the victim with bodily injury (but not actually causing the injury)
3. Physically contacting the victim in a way that the offender knows will be considered offensive or provocative.

One of the key elements of this crime is the culpable mental state of the offender. The law allows for the crime of assault when an actual injury was committed intentionally, knowingly, or recklessly. If the assault consisted of a threat of injury or of offensive or provocative physical contact, the offender's mental state must be at the level of intentional or knowing.

In most cases, assault that involves involving actual physical harm to the victim is a Class A misdemeanor. However, according to Pen §22.02, the crime becomes a third degree felony if the victim falls into one of the following categories:

- the victim is a public servant and the assault was committed while he/she is involved in lawful official duties or in retaliation for the performance of such duties

- the victim is a member of the offender's family or household and the offender has a prior conviction for assault against a member of his/her family or household

This second condition is a new change in the Penal Code; prior to September 1, 1999, repeat family violence of this type was elevated only to a state jail felony, not a third degree felony. In addition, the elevation of punishment used to require at least two prior convictions; currently one prior conviction or a deferred adjudication will lead to the enhanced punishment.

Assault that involves offensive touching or the threat of bodily harm is generally a Class C misdemeanor. However, the crime becomes a Class A misdemeanor if the victim is disabled or at least 65 years of age.

Aggravated assault is defined in Pen §22.02(a), which states that

> A person commits an offense if the person commits assault as defined in Section 22.01 and the person:
> (1) causes serious bodily injury to another, including the person's spouse; or
> (2) uses or exhibits a deadly weapon during the commission of the assault.

Essentially, this crime is simple assault with the presence of one of two additional aggravating elements, either the infliction of serious bodily harm or the use or exhibition of a deadly weapon while committing the assault. A 1994 revision of this statute added the element of exhibiting a deadly weapon; prior to that time, only the actual use of a deadly weapon was sufficient to elevate the crime from simple to aggravated assault.

Because of the first condition (serious bodily injury), there is often a very fine line between simple and aggravated assault, depending on the exact nature of the injury sustained by the victim.. There is a considerable amount of case law in Texas discussing the definition of serious bodily injury.

In most cases, aggravated assault is a second degree felony. However, as with simple assault, penalty enhancements are provided for in certain situations. The crime becomes a first degree felony if one of the following conditions applies:

- the offender is a public servant who is acting under color of his/her office
- the victim is a public servant and the assault was committed while he/she is involved in lawful official duties or in retaliation for the performance of such duties

- the victim was assaulted because he/she served as a witness, prospective witness, or informant, or because he/she reported a crime

BURGLARY

In common law, the crime of **burglary** was defined as the breaking and entering of a dwelling at night with intent to commit a felony. Today, the definition of burglary includes structures other than a dwelling place, can occur during the daytime as well as at night, and can involve either an intended felony or misdemeanor. The UCR defines burglary as the "unlawful entry of a structure to commit a felony or theft." Schmalleger discusses burglary on pp.48-49.

In Texas, burglary statutes are found in Chapter 30 of the Penal Code. According to Pen §30.02(a):

> A person commits an offense if, without the effective consent of the owner, he:
> (1) enters a habitation, or a building (or any portion of a building) not then open to the public, with intent to commit a felony, theft, or an assault; or
> (2) remains concealed, with intent to commit a felony, theft, or an assault, in a building or habitation; or
> (3) enters a building or habitation and commits or attempts to commit a felony, theft, or an assault.

The level of intent required varies with the sections of the statute. For the first type of burglary, the state must prove entry with specific intent to commit a felony, theft, or assault. For the other two types of burglary, the state is not required to prove that the offender, at the time he/she entered the building or habitation, had specific intent to commit the underlying crime. However, for the second type of burglary listed above, the state must show that the offender remained hidden in the location with the intent to commit the felony, theft, or assault.

The actual conduct also varies with the sections of the statute. For the first two types of burglary, the actual felony, theft, or assault does not have to actually take place and the state is not required to prove the elements of the underlying crime. However, for the third type of burglary the state must prove that the underlying crime was actually committed or attempted.

Several types of burglary include the element of entry. Entry occurs when any part of the offender's body or any physical object that is connected with the offender's body crosses or intrudes into the plane of the structure. Presence just outside a door does not constitute entry. However, reaching an arm or something held in the hand through a window is sufficient to establish entry. Unlawful entry occurs when the defendant is not licensed or privileged to enter. A defendant who remains concealed unlawfully may have originally entered the premises legally but remains after the termination of this legal right (e.g., a shoplifter who enters a store while it is open to the public but remains in the store after closing hours).

For the crime to be considered a burglary under Texas laws, the location must be a building or a habitation. Pen §30.01 defines these terms:

> (1) "Habitation" means a structure or vehicle that is adapted for the overnight accommodation of persons, and includes:
> (A) each separately secured or occupied portion of the structure or vehicle; and
> (B) each structure appurtenant to or connected with the structure or vehicle.
> (2) "Building" means any enclosed structure intended for use or occupation as a habitation or for some purpose of trade, manufacture, ornament, or use.
> (3) "Vehicle" includes any device in, on, or by which any person or property is or may be propelled, moved, or drawn in the normal course of commerce or transportation, except such devices as are classified as "habitation."

The penalty for burglary depends on the characteristics of the crime. The burglary of a building that is not a habitation (e.g., a business of some type) is a state jail felony. The burglary of a habitation with intent to steal is a second degree felony. The burglary of a habitation with intent to commit (or the actual commission of) a non-theft felony (e.g., an assault) is a first degree felony.

The Texas Penal Code also recognizes two other specific types of burglary, which do not involve buildings or habitations. Pen §30.03(a) discusses the burglary of coin-operated or coin collection machines. According to the statute:

> A person commits an offense if, without the effective consent of the owner, he breaks or enters into any coin-operated machine, coin collection machine, or other coin-operated or coin collection receptacle, contrivance, apparatus, or equipment used for the purpose of providing lawful amusement, sales of goods, services, or other valuable things, or telecommunications with intent to obtain property or services.

This crime is a Class A misdemeanor.

In addition, Pen §30.04(a) defines the burglary of a vehicle, stating that:

> A person commits an offense if, without the effective consent of the owner, he breaks into or enters a vehicle or any part of a vehicle with intent to commit any felony or theft.

In most cases, this crime is a Class A misdemeanor. However, if the vehicle or part of vehicle that was broken into was a rail car, or a container or trailer carried on a rail car, the crime is a state jail felony. The term "vehicle" was defined in Pen §30.01(3) and includes not only automobiles but also items such as trucks, buses, railway cars, golf carts, and mobile homes that have not been secured for use as habitation.

LARCENY-THEFT

Schmalleger discusses the crime of larceny on pp.49-50. The FBI defines **larceny-theft** as:

> the unlawful taking, carrying, leading, or riding away of property from the possession or constructive possession of another. It includes crimes such as shoplifting, pocket-picking, purse-snatching, thefts from motor vehicles, thefts of motor vehicle parts and accessories, bicycle thefts, etc., in which no use of force, violence, or fraud occurs.

In Texas, a number of crimes, including theft, theft by false pretext, conversion by a bailee, theft from the person, shoplifting acquisition of property by threat, swindling, swindling by worthless check, embezzlement, extortion, receiving or concealing embezzled property, and receiving or concealing stolen property were consolidated into the single crime of "theft" by Pen §31.02

Pen §31.03, which discusses the crime of theft, is extremely long and somewhat awkward. The offense itself is defined in section (a), which states that a theft occurs when a person "unlawfully appropriates property with intent to deprive the owner of property." Essentially, the crime has two elements:

1. The offender must appropriate the property unlawfully
2. The offender must have intent to deprive the owner of the property.

The statute outlines when appropriation of property is unlawful. According to section (b) of the statute, this occurs when one of the following conditions is met:

1. The property is taken without the owner's consent
2. The offender knowingly appropriates property that was stolen by another person (this is essentially the old "receiving stolen property" statute and allows the state to more easily prosecute offenders for fencing)

3. The property is in the custody of a law enforcement agency, a law enforcement agent specifically told the offender the property was stolen, and the offender appropriates the property while believing it was stolen by another person.

The penalty for the crime of theft depends primarily on the value of the property that was stolen. According to Pen §31.03(e), theft is:

(1) a Class C misdemeanor if the value of the property stolen is less than:
  (A) $50; or
  (B) $20 and the defendant obtained the property by issuing or passing a check or similar sight order...;
(2) a Class B misdemeanor if:
  (A) the value of the property stolen is:
    (i) $50 or more but less than $500; or
    (ii) $20 or more but less than $500 and the defendant obtained the property by issuing or passing a check or similar sight order...; or
  (B) the value of the property stolen is less than:
    (i) $50 and the defendant has previously been convicted of any grade of theft; or
    (ii) $20, the defendant has previously been convicted of any grade of theft, and the defendant obtained the property by issuing or passing a check or similar sight order...;
(3) a Class A misdemeanor if the value of the property stolen is $500 or more but less than $1,500;
(4) a state jail felony if:
  (A) the value of the property stolen is $1,500 or more but less than $20,000, or the property is less than 10 head of cattle, horses, or exotic livestock or exotic fowl as defined by Section 142.001, Agriculture Code, or any part thereof under the value of $20,000, or less than 100 head of sheep, swine, or goats or any part thereof under the value of $20,000;
  (B) regardless of value, the property is stolen from the person of another or from a human corpse or grave;
  (C) the property stolen is a firearm...; or
  (D) the value of the property stolen is less than $1,500 and the defendant has been previously convicted two or more times of any grade of theft;
(5) a felony of the third degree if the value of the property stolen is $20,000 or more but less than $100,000, or the property is:
  (A) 10 or more head of cattle, horses, or exotic livestock or exotic fowl as defined by Section 142.001, Agriculture Code, stolen during a single transaction and having an aggregate value of less than $100,000; or
  (B) 100 or more head of sheep, swine, or goats stolen during a single transaction and having an aggregate value of less than $100,000;

(6) a felony of the second degree if the value of the property stolen is $100,000 or more but less than $200,000; or
(7) a felony of the first degree if the value of the property stolen is $200,000 or more.

In addition, any theft will be increased by one level if it can be shown that the offender was a public servant or government contractor and that the offender obtained the property because of this status.

According to Pen §31.01(5), property can include any of the following:

(A) real property;
(B) tangible or intangible personal property including anything severed from land; or
(C) a document, including money, that represents or embodies anything of value.

In a separate statute (Pen §31.04), Texas also recognized the crime of theft of service, which involves:

(a) A person commits theft of service if, with intent to avoid payment for service that he knows is provided only for compensation:
  (1) he intentionally or knowingly secures performance of the service by deception, threat, or false token;
  (2) having control over the disposition of services of another to which he is not entitled, he intentionally or knowingly diverts the other's services to his own benefit or to the benefit of another not entitled to them; or
  (3) having control of personal property under a written rental agreement, he holds the property beyond the expiration of the rental period without the effective consent of the owner of the property, thereby depriving the owner of the property of its use in further rentals.

The main purpose of this statute is to outlaw the unlawful taking of something that does not fall under the definition of property as outlined above. Service is defined in Pen §31.01(6) and includes labor and professional services, various public utility, transportation, and telecommunication services, lodging, restaurant service, entertainment, and property rental. As with theft of property, the seriousness of this crime is determined by the value of the service stolen:

- The crime is a Class C misdemeanor if the value is less than $20
- The crime is a Class B misdemeanor if the value is at least $20 but less than $500
- The crime is a Class A misdemeanor if the value is at least $500 but less than $1,500
- The crime is a state jail felony if the value is at least $1,500 but less than $20,000
- The crime is a third degree felony if the value is at least $20,00 but less than $100,000

- The crime is a second degree felony if the value is at least $100,000 but less than $200,000
- The crime is a first degree felony if the value is at least $200,000

MOTOR VEHICLE THEFT

The UCR considers **motor vehicle theft** to be a separate index crime from larceny-theft. Schmalleger discusses this crime on p.50. It is defined by the FBI as:

> the theft or attempted theft of a motor vehicle, this offense category includes the stealing of automobiles, trucks, buses, motorcycles, motorscooters, snowmobiles, etc.

Texas does not consider motor vehicle theft to be a separate crime from theft. The statutory definition of theft (Pen §31.03) includes the theft of any tangible personal property; this would include the theft of a motor vehicle.

In addition, Pen §31.07 discusses the crime of the **unauthorized use of a vehicle**. The statute states that:

> (a) A person commits an offense if he intentionally or knowingly operates another's boat, airplane, or motor-propelled vehicle without the effective consent of the owner.

This statute effectively outlaws "joyriding." Actual operation of the vehicle is an element of the crime; merely entering the vehicle without the owner's consent does not meet the statutory definition of the crime. The crime is a state jail felony.

ARSON

Like burglary, the common-law felony crime of **arson** was a crime against a home or dwelling place. While it could occur at any time of day, nighttime arson was considered to be a more serious crime. Schmalleger discusses the crime of arson on p.51. The UCR defines arson as:

> any willful or malicious burning or attempt to burn, with or without intent to defraud, a dwelling house, public building, motor vehicle or aircraft, personal property of another, etc.

In Texas, arson against structures other than a home and the burning of other types of property is also recognized. Pen §28.01 defines the crime of arson, stating that:

> (a) A person commits an offense if he starts a fire or causes an explosion with intent to destroy or damage:
> (1) any vegetation, fence, or structure on open-space land; or
> (2) any building, habitation, or vehicle:

(A) knowing that it is within the limits of an incorporated city or town;
(B) knowing that it is insured against damage or destruction;
(C) knowing that it is subject to a mortgage or other security interest;
(D) knowing that it is located on property belonging to another;
(E) knowing that it has located within it property belonging to another; or
(F) when he is reckless about whether the burning or explosion will endanger the life of some individual or the safety of the property of another.

(b) It is an exception to the application of Subsection (a)(1) that the fire or explosion was a part of the controlled burning of open-space land.

Building, habitation, and vehicle are defined the same way as for the crime of burglary.

According to the definition of the crime, a key element of the crime of arson is specific intent to destroy or damage some type of property. Therefore, careless behavior that results in a fire (e.g., shooting off fireworks during a drought) is not arson under the statute. In addition, obtaining a permit for a fire from the state prior to starting the fire is a defense against prosecution for the crime of arson.

In most cases, arson is a second degree felony. However, the crime is elevated to a first degree felony if one of the two conditions applies. First, if the offense resulted in bodily injury or death to any person, the crime is considered to be more serious. The definition of bodily injury has been debated in the courts and may even include smoke inhalation. Second, if the offender committed the crime knowing that the property targeted was a place of worship. This condition was added in 1997 after a number of churches throughout Texas and other southern states were burned.

HATE CRIMES

Schmalleger (pp.53-56) discusses the issue of **hate crimes**. He defines a hate crime as:

> A criminal offense in which the motive was hatred, bias, or prejudice, based on the actual or perceived race, color, religion, national origin, ethnicity, gender, or sexual orientation of another individual or group of individuals.

While hate crimes are not specifically included in the UCR's eight index crimes, the FBI began to collect data on this category of crime after President Bush signed the Hate Crimes Statistics Act in 1990.

Section 411.046 of the Government Code, the Texas Hate Crime Reporting Act, defines hate crimes as "crimes that are motivated by prejudice, hatred, or advocacy of violence..." The Act requires all law enforcement agencies in Texas to report hate or bias crimes to the Texas Department of Public Safety (DPS); the DPS is required to maintain and disseminate records and statistics on hate crimes in the state.

According to the DPS annual report on Crime in Texas, there were a total of 267 hate crime incidents reported in Texas in 1999, a decrease of 15.5 percent over 1998. The 267 reported hate crime incidents in 1999 resulted in a total of 286 reported offenses. Most of these (approximately 96 percent) involved simple assault (24 percent); aggravated assault (15 percent); intimidation (29 percent); and vandalism (28 percent).

The most frequent motivation was racial; approximately 58 percent of the reported hate crimes were by the race or color of the victim. Other motivations included the victim's sexual orientation (22 percent); religion (10 percent); and ethnicity or national origin (8 percent). There were a small number of hate crimes (less than 1 percent) motivated by the victim's disability.

The 286 reported offenses involved a total of 302 offenders, 262 victims, and 286 reported offenses in 1999. The majority of hate crime offenders were white (approximately 56 percent). Approximately 10 percent were black. However, the race of almost 32 percent of hate crime offenders was unknown in 1999. The most common victim was an individual; over 70 percent of all hate crimes were directed against individual victims.

Texas' "hate crimes law" is found in Pen §12.47, which mandates sentencing enhancements if a crime was committed because of bias or prejudice. The statute states that:

> If the court makes an affirmative finding under Article 42.015, Code of Criminal Procedure, in the punishment phase of the trial of an offense under Chapter 29, Chapter 31, or Title 5, other than a first degree felony or a Class A misdemeanor, the punishment for the offense is increased to the punishment prescribed for the next highest category of offense. If the offense is a Class A misdemeanor, the minimum term of confinement for the offense is increased to 180 days.

Essentially, if it can be shown that the victim was selected primarily because the defendant had some bias or prejudice against a specific group, this statute applies. Unfortunately, the term "group" is not defined either in the Penal Law or in the Code of Criminal Procedure, making the application of this law somewhat difficult and vague.

CHAPTER 4

THE POLICE IN TEXAS

INTRODUCTION

Schmalleger (see Chapter 5) discusses the topic of the various levels of law enforcement in the United States today. It is clear that there are many levels of police agencies in America, including federal law enforcement, state police, county sheriffs' agencies, and city police.

Texas' location, particularly its proximity to Mexico, creates a number of special law enforcement problems, including issues such as drugs, immigration, and tourism. Because of this, a large number of federal law enforcement agencies have offices in Texas and/or are involved in law enforcement activities within the state. This includes the Federal Bureau of Investigation; the Drug Enforcement Agency; the Immigration and Naturalization Service U.S. Customs; the Bureau of Alcohol, Tobacco, and Firearms; the U.S. Coast Guard; and the U.S. Border Patrol. This results in a considerable amount of overlap among the various levels of law enforcement in the state. See Schmalleger (pp.177-180) for a discussion of some of the key federal law enforcement agencies in the United States.

LOCAL POLICING

Schmalleger (see p.183) briefly discusses the topic of **local policing** in the United States. The majority of police departments in Texas are local or city departments. Currently, most local cities, towns, and villages in Texas maintain police departments. Every local department is independent of every other department. The goals, purposes, and priorities vary greatly among departments, with each local agency responding to the needs and desires of the population it serves. Sizes range from small departments with less than five full-time officers to large urban agencies with thousands of sworn officers.

Municipal police departments in Texas are full-service police agencies which provide a wide range of police services, including law enforcement, order maintenance, and service. The chief or director of each department generally is appointed by the head of the city's political system.

The Houston Police Department

Houston is the largest city in the state of Texas. The **Houston Police Department** (HPD) was established in 1841. Currently, the HPD is the largest police department in Texas; in 1999 the department employed 5,443 sworn officers and 1,948 civilians.

The department is divided into eight "Commands," each with a specific area of responsibility:

- North Patrol Command

- South Patrol Command
- Investigations Command
- Information Services Command
- Professional Development Command
- Technical Services Command
- Tactical Support Command
- Support Services Command

The **North Patrol Command** and the **South Patrol Command** provide basic patrol services to specific areas of the city. Officers assigned to these commands respond to emergencies and to citizen calls for service, conduct preliminary investigations at crime scenes, investigate accidents, and enforce the city's traffic laws. The **Investigations Command** is the Department's detective bureau. It investigates crimes, locates and apprehends suspects, locates missing persons, and recovers stolen property. The Command is divided into a number of specialized divisions to investigate specific types of crimes such as homicide, robbery, burglary and theft, vice, auto theft, juvenile crimes, narcotics, and hate crimes.

The **Information Services Command** provides a variety of support services to the HPD, including records, planning and research, crime analysis, communications, and computer services. It is also responsible for applying for, and administering, government grants. The Emergency Communications Division of the Command is the department's dispatching center; it receives all calls for service, prioritizes them, and dispatches patrol officers to each call. The Command also includes the Inspections Division, which has among its duties the development of departmental standard operating procedures. Personnel matters are handled by the **Professional Development Command**, which is responsible for tasks such as recruitment, hiring, initial and in-service training, psychological services, and personnel development. The Police Chaplain is a member of this Command.

The **Technical Services Command** has three divisions. The Identification Division includes a variety of laboratories (such as fingerprint, firearms, and voice imaging enhancement). It also collects and maintains criminal history data for all suspects who have been arrested for a crime that is at least a Class B misdemeanor. The Crime Lab Division is responsible for scientific analysis of evidence and for providing technical assistance to officers at major crime scenes. This division also includes a photographic laboratory. The Jail Division oversees the HPD jail, which houses all prisoners arrested by the HPD as well as some other local law enforcement agencies. During 1998, approximately 119,000 prisoners were booked into Houston's three jails, which include the Central Jail, the Southeast Jail, and the Municipal Detention Center (which houses male prisoners who were sentenced to jail time rather than fines by the Municipal Courts). Many special situations, such as traffic accidents, the protection of local and visiting dignitaries, and security at special events, are handled by the **Tactical Support Command**. Other responsibilities of this Command include patrolling and responding to citizen calls for service in the city's Central Business District, participating in accident investigations, and recovering evidence and property from under water. Finally, the **Support Services Command** is responsible for the management of department facilities and property, including all HPD vehicles.

Currently, the minimum entry requirements for the HPD include:

- U.S. citizen
- must be between the ages of 21 and 35
- weight proportionate to height
- must have at least 60 semester hours from an accredited college or university with a minimum 2.0 GPA or an honorable military discharge
- valid driver's licence and proof of liability insurance
- no felony convictions
- no more than two moving violation convictions within the past 18 months
- stable credit history
- individuals with a prior military background must not have been convicted of any court-martial higher than a summary.

The selection process lasts an average of about six months and all applicants must successfully complete each of ten phases to qualify for the police academy. The hiring process includes:

- complete preliminary questionnaire and interview
- complete HPD application paperwork
- reading comprehension test
- work sample test (physical agility)
- polygraph examination
- final interview
- fingerprints and photographs
- background investigation
- medical examination and drug testing
- psychological testing and evaluation

After the applicant has completed the first eight steps (i.e;, through the background investigation), he/she may be given a conditional job offer. After successfully completing the medical and psychological examinations, applicants enter the academy as positions become available. Cadets attend a 24-week academy training program, followed by time in the Officer Field Training Program. In 1999, Police Cadets in the academy received a base salary of $26,024.70. Probationary officers received a base salary of $27,616.94, and first-year officers received a base salary of $29,925.48. All first-year and above officers also receive a $1,200 equipment allowance. Officers with college degrees also receive a salary increase: $2,600 for a bachelor's degree, $5,200 for a master's degree, and $7,800 for a doctoral degree.

The Dallas Police Department

The **Dallas Police Department** (DPD) has a total of 3,572 employees. Of these, 2,845 are sworn officers and 727 are non-sworn civilian employees. During the 1997-1998 fiscal year, the department had an annual budget of $229,407,769; over $212 million of this was allocated for salaries and the rest for operating expenses. During 1997, the department handled over 943,000 calls for police service.

The department is divided into three main sections, each with a variety of special divisions. The **Uniformed Sections** have a variety of responsibilities. The patrol division responds to citizen calls for service and conducts preliminary crime scene investigations. The tactical division includes the department's S.W.A.T. team, whereas the traffic section is involved in traffic enforcement and investigates accidents and all crimes related to vehicles. Finally, 72 officers are assigned to the department's Interactive Community Policing (ICP) program

There are a number of divisions within the DPD's **Detective Sections**. The General Investigations Division is responsible for investigating crimes such as auto theft, financial crimes, computer crimes, forgery, pawn shop transactions, and swindles. The Narcotics Division investigates narcotics and money laundering offenses. The Patrol Division is composed of patrol investigative units assigned to each patrol area; these units investigate property crimes that occur within that area. Other areas within the Detective Sections include the vice unit, the public integrity unit (which investigates crimes committed by City of Dallas employees), the Internal Affairs Division (which investigates officers for violations of departmental rules and regulations), CAPERS (which investigates crimes against persons), and the youth and family crimes division.

The department's **Support Services Section** is responsible for recruiting and training of new officers. This section runs the DPD Academy and provides both pre-service and in-service training.

Currently, the minimum entry requirements for the DPD include:

- a minimum of 45 semester hours from an accredited university or college with at least a "C" average
- must be at least 21 years of age, or 19.5 years of age with at least 60 semester hours at a "C" average or better
- must be a U.S. citizen
- no felony convictions
- an honorable discharge from the military (if applicable)
- a valid driver's license

Applicants who meet these minimum criteria must then go through the following eight phases in the hiring process:

- preliminary interview
- civil service test
- physical agility test
- polygraph examination
- background investigation
- applicant interview board
- psychological evaluation
- medical evaluation

Those applicants who receive appointments as Trainee Police Officers go through a 32-week training program at the Dallas Police Academy, followed by a 24-week period with a field training officer. Trainee officers receive a base salary of $28,498; this increases to $28,969 during field training and

$29,142 during the probationary period. The base starting salary for police officers is $29,919. Special pay options include educational incentive pay (with officers completing a bachelor's degree receiving an additional $100 per month in salary), language pay for officers fluent in sign language, Spanish, Cambodian, or Laotian, shift differential pay for officers working at least 50 percent of their scheduled work hours between 6 p.m. and 6 a.m., longevity pay, service incentive pay, and patrol duty pay for officers in patrol, traffic, or special operations division.

COUNTY POLICING

Schmalleger covers the topic of **county sheriffs' departments** in the United States in his discussion of local agencies (see p.183). There are 254 counties in Texas, each with a separate sheriff's department. The Texas Constitution (Article 5, Section 23) states that the sheriff of each county will be elected by the qualified voters of the county in a general election. All sheriffs serve terms of four years. Therefore, partisan politics significantly influences county police agencies in the state. According to Article 16, Section 61, of the Texas Constitution, all sheriffs, deputy sheriffs, and other county law enforcement officers must be paid on a salary basis, rather than a fee basis.

Most sheriff's departments in Texas are full-service police agencies that provide police services to all unincorporated areas of the county. In addition, incorporated towns or cities that do not wish to set up their own local police department may contract out to their county sheriff's department for police services. In most counties, there are no mandatory minimum training requirements which must be met by candidates running for sheriff. For example, candidates for sheriff are not required to have attended a police academy or to have any practical policing experience of any kind.

In many counties, the sheriff's department is not only responsible for providing law enforcement services to the county but also for running the county jail, maintaining security in all county courts, serving civil and criminal processes, and providing assistance when needed to local departments within the county. This assistance can range from operating a county-wide crime lab to assisting a local department with a criminal investigation. County sheriffs have police powers throughout the county, including within the boundaries of incorporated cities that maintain a city police force. In addition, according to Article 8, Section 16 of the Texas Constitution:

> The Sheriff of each county, in addition to his other duties, shall be the Assessor and Collector of Taxes therefor...

The Harris County Sheriff's Department

Harris County, TX, is the third-largest county in the entire country. It has an area of 1,788 square miles and a population of over 3 million. Located in southeast Texas, the county includes the city of Houston. The **Harris County Sheriff's Department** (HCSD), which is one of the oldest law enforcement agencies in the state, was founded in 1837 with one mounted officer. Currently, the department has approximately 3,500 employees.

The HCSD is divided into eight bureaus, each headed by an officer with the rank of major:

- Patrol
- Detective
- Human Resources
- Technical Services
- Medical Services
- Planning and Evaluation
- Inmate Housing (701)
- Inmate Housing (1301)

The **Patrol Bureau** provides law enforcement services to unincorporated areas in Harris county. There are four main patrol districts as well as the Central Patrol Division, which includes traffic enforcement, the crime prevention unit, D.A.R.E., the department's mounted and marine patrols, and the Citizen's Police Academy. Deputies assigned to the patrol bureau are involved in criminal investigations, arrest offenders, enforce traffic laws, and investigate traffic accidents.

The **Detective Bureau** is the criminal investigation unit of the HCSD. It is composed of 11 specialized divisions, including Crimes Against Persons, Crimes Against Property, Auto Theft, the Organized Crime and Narcotics Task Force, Internal Affairs, and the Youth Gang Intervention Unit. To be eligible for assignment to the detective bureau, a deputy must have been working for the HCSD for at least 18 months and pass the department's civil service examination for promotion to the rank of detective.

The **Human Resources Bureau** is responsible for recruitment and training, background investigations, inventory, payroll, bookkeeping, accreditation, and minority affairs. This bureau also runs the Harris County Sheriff's Academy, which includes approximately 720 hours of training.

The department's **Technical Services Bureau** provides a variety of support services to the HCSD. The Bureau's Communications Division handles all calls for service that come from unincorporated Harris County. The ID/AFIS Division is responsible for the Automated Fingerprint Identification System as well as maintaining criminal history information on all offender who are charged with at least a Class B misdemeanor in the county. The Systems Division deals with the development and maintenance of all computers and networks within the department. Finally, the Bureau's Alarm, Property, and Report's Division is responsible for regulating alarm use, storing and processing all found property and evidence, maintaining offense records of criminal incidents, and preparing the Harris County Uniform Crime Reports.

The **Medical Services Bureau** provides medical services to all inmates who are housed in HCSD detention facilities. The Bureau provides a wide variety of services including 24-hour on-call physician services, nursing services, dental services, pharmacy, laboratory, and radiology services, HIV counseling, substance abuse services, and dietary services. Each month, the staff of the Medical Services Bureau see approximately 32,000 inmates and fill approximately 10,000 prescriptions.

The **Planning and Evaluation Bureau** has seven main divisions, all of which are involved in some way with inmate custody. The Court Division is responsible for court security. The Detention

Training Section provides pre-service and in-service training for detention deputies as well as assisting the Sheriff's Academy when needed. The Inmate Education Section provides educational opportunities for inmates, allowing them to complete their G.E.D. and to obtain job skills in a variety of areas. The Bureau's Inmate Processing Center (IPC) processes prisoners in and out of the county jail system; in any given 24-hour period, the IPC processes approximately 300 new prisoners and releases approximately 250 inmates. The Laundry, Kitchen, and Commissary Section is responsible for laundry in the jails, the distribution of cleaning supplies, providing food service to all inmates, and the running of the jail commissary. Inmate jail records are maintained by the Central Records, Bonding, and Fines section, which also process bonds, investigates bonding companies in Harris County, and collect all court-ordered payments, such as fines and court costs. Finally, the transportation division moves inmates from the county jails to hospitals, courts, medical appointments, and the state penitentiary.

There are two inmate housing bureaus in the HCSD. The **701 Inmate Housing Bureau** is one of the largest detention facilities in the US, with 4,000 permanent beds and space for up to 500 temporary beds. It has been in operation since 1991. The **1301 Inmate Housing Bureau**, which is located in downtown Houston, is a maximum-security institution. It has 409 beds for inmate workers as well as housing most court holdovers (approximately 800-900 inmates per day).

The Jefferson County Sheriff's Department

Jefferson County, which has an area of approximately 975 square miles, is located in southeast Texas. The **Jefferson County Sheriff's Department** (JCSD) is divided into three main divisions. The **Law Enforcement Division** provides a wide variety of law enforcement services to county residents. It includes patrol, criminal investigations, D.A.R.E., a street crimes unit, a S.W.A.T. team, auto theft and narcotics task forces, the department's communication division (which processes all calls for service), identification, and internal affairs. The Division's training unit runs the Sheriff's Peace Officer Academy, which serves all local law enforcement agencies within the county as well as JCSD law enforcement and correctional officers. The Academy provides approximately 700 hours of pre-service training to cadets, as well as a variety of in-service training programs.

The **Corrections Division** is responsible for running the Jefferson County Correctional Facility, which houses individuals awaiting trial as well as inmates sentenced to short-term incarceration in a county facility. Finally, the **Services Division** provides a variety of special and support services to the Department. Special services include the Airborne Extradition Unit, the K-9 Unit, and the Aviation Unit (which operates helicopters to supplement ground patrol officers). The division is also responsible for support services, such as personnel, recruitment, maintenance and preservation of property and evidence, and for running the regional crime laboratory.

Minimum entry standards for the JCSD include:

- be at least 21 years of age
- live within a 50-mile radius of the Jefferson County Courthouse
- have a valid Texas driver's licence, a good driving record, and proof of valid automobile insurance

- have an AA degree (60 credit hours) or be willing to sign a probation extension which states that the applicant will achieve an AA degree within five years
- have no felony convictions
- have no convictions of a Class A or B misdemeanor, a DWI or a DUI in the last 5 years

The application process includes eight main steps:

- Preliminary Screening
- Written examination (reading comprehension/vocabulary test and spelling test)
- Background investigation
- Polygraph examination
- Psychological examination and interview
- Interview with the deputy chief
- Interview with the sheriff
- Agility test and drug screening

The entry-level salary for a sheriff's deputy is $2,334 per month. The entry-level salary for correctional officers is $1,857 per month. Educational incentive pay is also available.

STATE POLICING

Schmalleger (see pp.180-183) discusses **state police agencies** within the United States. Some states, such as California, have two agencies, one to conduct criminal investigations and a separate uniformed highway patrol. However, other states, including Texas, operate one full-service state police agency which includes both highway patrol functions and criminal investigation.

The Texas Department of Public Safety

On August 10, 1935, the state legislature created the **Texas Department of Public Safety** (DPS) as a statewide law enforcement agency. The former Texas Highway Patrol was incorporated into this new agency. The Department's stated mission is "to maintain public safety in the State of Texas."

The DPS is divided into six major divisions:

- Administration
- Director's Staff
- Driver's Licenses
- Criminal Law Enforcement
- Traffic Law Enforcement
- Texas Rangers

The **Administration Division** is the staff support services arm of the DPS, providing administrative support to all other divisions within the Department. It maintains crime records and fingerprint files, operates the DPS Training Academy, is responsible for various personnel programs and functions, is in charge of the Department's fleet of vehicles, and provides a variety of other staff support functions. This division is also responsible for Texas emergency management services. The division's UCR program collects data on crimes reported to or known to the police, provides data to the FBI's national UCR program, and publishes state crime statistics twice a year.

The **Director's Staff**, which includes the Director of the DPS and two Assistant Directors, is responsible for overseeing all DPS functions. Several sections report directly to the director and assistant directors of the DPS, including Public Information, Accounting, Aircraft, Internal Affairs, Information Management, and General Counsel.

The **Drivers License Division** issues and controls all drivers licenses in Texas. Division responsibilities include testing new drivers, voter registration, and improvement and control of problem drivers.

The **Criminal Law Enforcement Division** (CLE) focuses on law enforcement activities and provides specialized assistance not only to DPS officers but also to other law enforcement agencies throughout Texas. Currently, the CLE Division includes 946 individuals, of which 527 are commissioned officers. The CLE is involved in a wide variety of multi-jurisdictional investigations, working with municipal, county, state, and federal agencies to combat crimes such as narcotics, motor vehicle theft, fraud, gambling, and public corruption. There are five units or "services" within the CLE Division, each of which focuses on a specific function. The Narcotics Service is responsible for directing the statewide attempts to deter and eliminate illegal drug trafficking, supervising the registration of controlled substances, administering prescription requirements for certain controlled substances (known as Schedule II controlled substances), and supervising the state's precursor chemical program (which controls chemicals that may be used in the illegal manufacture of drugs such as amphetamine and methamphetamine.) The Motor Vehicle Theft Service focuses specifically on motor vehicle theft in Texas, including control, deterrence, and vehicle recovery. In 1996, the state was ranked third in the U.S. in this crime, with a theft loss of almost $634 million. The Special Crimes Service has a wide variety of functions and duties, including general criminal investigation, information gathering, providing assistance to the Governor's Protective Detail when the governor travels officially within the state, administration of a variety of regulatory programs (e.g., sex offender registration), and performing background investigations not only of possible DPS employees but of applicants to sensitive positions in other state agencies. The Polygraph Service conducts polygraph examinations of suspects, witnesses, and victims for law enforcement agencies throughout the state to assist in criminal investigations. This service also provides training in polygraph operation to law enforcement personnel. Finally, the Crime Laboratory Service provides forensic laboratory services to law enforcement agencies throughout Texas.

The **Traffic Law Enforcement Division** (TLE) is responsible for enforcing the law on Texas highways. It includes six main services. The Highway Patrol Service patrols rural highways in Texas, enforcing both traffic and criminal law. Currently, the Highway Patrol has an authorized strength of 1,703 troopers. The License and Weights Service enforces laws that relate to commercial vehicles and commercial drivers licenses (e.g., size, weight, and registration of commercial vehicles) as well as enforcing all traffic laws relating to commercial vehicles. The Vehicle Inspection Service is responsible for conducting emissions testing and general vehicle inspections of vehicles in Texas. The Safety Education Service is responsible for educating the public in Texas traffic laws and traffic safety. Topics of importance include child safety seat use, seat belt use, bicycle safety, pedestrian safety, crime prevention, drug and DWI awareness, and basic traffic safety. In 1998 alone, the Service conducted over 17,000 safety presentations to the public as well as 283 classes for police agencies throughout the state. The Communications Service operates a statewide network serving the communications needs of criminal justice agencies throughout Texas. For example, police officers requesting driver's license status and vehicle registration information go through the DPS Communications Service. The service also is widely used by members of the public requesting police assistance. Finally, the Capitol Police is responsible for the safety and security of the Capitol Complex, a 46-square block area in downtown Austin with a daytime population of approximately 40,000 people; the Complex includes not only the State Capitol Building, but also 28 state office buildings, 27 garages and parking lots, and 15 private office buildings. The Capitol Police protect the complex, assist visitors, control traffic, supervise parking, and conduct investigations of any crimes occurring within the complex. They also provide protection for visiting dignitaries as well as being responsible for security at the Texas Governor's Mansion.

Finally, the **Texas Rangers Division** is one of the oldest law enforcement agencies in the U.S. It focuses primarily on the investigation of major felonies and other related crimes that are not the responsibility of other DPS Divisions (e.g., gambling is handled by the Special Crimes Division, drug crimes are handled by the Narcotics Service, and auto theft is the responsibility of the Motor Vehicle Theft Service). The Texas Rangers deal primarily with crimes such as murder, rape, robbery, burglary, white collar crime, and government corruption. In 1996, the Rangers conducted 3,680 investigations, resulting in 601 felony arrests; recovered over $3 million in stolen property; and seized over $1 million in contraband.

The minimum standards that must be met by all individuals applying to the DPS include:

- must be at least 20 years of age upon appointment
- must be a U.S. citizen
- must have a valid Texas driver license
- must pass a physical examination by a physician
- vision must be at least 20/200 uncorrected, with specified levels of correction by eyeglasses or contact lenses; applicant must also meet other specified visual criteria
- must have at least 60 semester hours from an accredited university or college, although prior law enforcement or military experience may substitute for educational requirements
- must be of good moral character and habits - applicants with a final conviction for any felony, DWI, DUID, or misdemeanor domestic violence offense will be automatically disqualified
- must have a good traffic record

The hiring process consists of the following stages for those applicants who meet the minimum requirements:

- Physical demands test, including measures of strength, the long jump, a 1.5 mile run, and a demonstration of gun proficience
- Written test, including reading comprehension and writing skills
- Background investigation
- Oral board interview

- Vision test
- Second physical demands test, including a 1.5 mile run (to be completed in 14 minutes or less), 40 sit-ups in one minute, and 25 push-ups in one minute
- Written psychological test
- Psychological interview
- Physical medical examination

Applicants who receive an invitation to the DPS Training Academy are required to live at the Academy during the training period, which lasts for 26 weeks. After completing the Academy, trooper-trainees are required to pass a written licensing examination which is administered by the Texas Commission on Law Enforcement Officer Standards and Education. As of September 1, 1999, trooper-trainees receive a salary of $2,000 per month while attending the DPS Academy. This is increased to 2,416.66 per month upon graduation and commission as a state trooper. Troopers who complete successfully complete six month probation receive a salary of $2,666.66 per month, and troopers who successfully complete the full 12-month probationary period are increased to $2,916.66 per month. Commissioned troopers may be assigned anywhere in the state.

The Texas Public Safety Commission

The **Texas Public Safety Commission** is responsible for overseeing the DPS. According to Government Code (GC) 411.003, the Commission includes three members who are appointed by the governor and confirmed by the Senate. They serve staggered six-year terms and receive no compensation for their service (although they may receive per diem for expenses).

GC 411.004 outlines the duties and powers of the Commission, stating that:

> The commission shall:
> (1) formulate plans and policies for:
> (A) enforcement of state criminal, traffic, and safety laws;
> (B) prevention of crime;
> (C) detection and apprehension of persons who violate laws; and
> (D) education of citizens of this state in the promotion of public safety and the observance of law;
> (2) organize the department and supervise its operation;
> (3) adopt rules considered necessary for carrying out the department's work;
> (4) maintain records of all proceedings and official orders;
> (5) biennially submit a report of its work to the governor and legislature, including the commission's and director's recommendations; and
> (6) provide to its members, as often as necessary, information regarding their qualifications for office under this chapter and their responsibilities under applicable laws relating to standards of conduct for state officers.

POLICE TRAINING

Police departments today require highly qualified and well-trained officers. Schmalleger (see pp.229-231) discusses the issue of professionalism and standards in the education and training of police officers. In Texas, the **Texas Commission on Law Enforcement Officer Standards and Education** (TCLEOSE), a state regulatory agency, establishes and maintains training standards for law enforcement and corrections officers in Texas. The Commission also develops training courses and monitors training programs throughout the state. TCLEOSE was established by GC 415.002.

TCLEOSE consists of a total of nine members who are appointed by the governor. They serve staggered six-year terms and receive no compensation for their service other than expenses. Of the nine members, three are law enforcement chief executive officers (e.g., a sheriff, constable, or chief of police), three are line personnel (in non-supervisory positions) from law enforcement agencies with at least five years experience, and three are members of the general public.

According to §217.1 of the Texas Administrative Code, the minimum standards that must be met to receive a license as a peace officer, armed public security officer, or jailer in Texas include:

(a) An applicant for a peace officer, a reserve, an armed public security officer, or a jailer license must:
  (1) meet the following minimum age requirements:
    (A) peace officer or reserve - 21 years of age, or 18 years of age if the applicant has received an associate's degree or 60 semester hours of credit from an accredited college or university or has received an honorable discharge from the armed forces of the United States after at least two years of active service;
    (B) armed public security officer - 21 years of age; or
    (C) jailer - 18 years of age;
  (2) be fingerprinted and be subjected to a search of local, state and national records and fingerprint files to disclose any criminal record;
  (3) not be on court-ordered community supervision or probation for any criminal offense above the grade of Class C misdemeanor;
  (4) not have been convicted of a misdemeanor offense above the grade of a Class C misdemeanor within the last five years ;
  (5) not have ever been convicted at any time of a felony offense;
  (6) not have ever been convicted of a misdemeanor or felony offense or placed on deferred adjudication community supervision for a misdemeanor or felony offense, if the offense directly relates to the duties and responsibilities of any office requiring such license. In determining whether a criminal offense directly relates to such office, the commission shall, under this subsection, consider:
    (A) the nature and seriousness of the crime;
    (B) the relationship of the crime to the purpose for requiring a license for such office;
    (C) the extent to which a license might offer an opportunity to engage in further criminal activity of the same type as that in which the person had previously been involved; and

(D) the relationship of the crime to the ability, capacity or fitness required to perform the duties and discharge the responsibilities of such office;

(7) be of good moral character;

(8) be subjected to a thorough, comprehensive background investigation and be interviewed personally prior to appointment by representatives of the appointing authority;

(9) meet one of the following minimum educational requirements:

(A) be a high school graduate;

(B) have passed a general educational development (GED) test indicating high school graduation level; or

(C) have 12 semester hours credit from an accredited college or university;

(10) be examined by a licensed physician and be declared in writing within 180 days before the date of employment by the agency both

(A) to be physically sound and free from any defect which may adversely affect the performance of duty appropriate to the type of license sought; and

(B) to show no trace of drug dependency or illegal drug use after a physical examination, blood test, or other medical test;

(11) be examined by a licensed psychologist or psychiatrist and be declared in writing by that professional within 180 days before the date of employment by the agency to be in satisfactory psychological and emotional health appropriate to the type of license sought and appointment to be made. The examination must be conducted pursuant to professionally recognized standards and methods, must be administered by an experienced professional who is a:

(A) licensed psychologist or psychiatrist, selected by the requesting agency;

(B) licensed physician recognized under exceptional circumstances; or

(C) qualified psychologist exempt from licensure by the Psychologist Certification and Licensing Act, Section 22, who is recognized under exceptional circumstances;

(12) not have been discharged from any military service under less than honorable conditions including, specifically;

(A) under other than honorable conditions;

(B) bad conduct;

(C) dishonorable; or

(D) any other characterization of service indicating bad character;

(13) not have had a commission license denied by final order or revoked, or have a voluntary surrender of license currently in effect;

(14) meet the minimum training standards and pass the commission licensing examination for each license sought;

(15) not violate any commission rule or provision of Texas Government Code annotated, Chapter 415.

TCLEOSE develops and maintains courses for preparatory training and continuing education of police officers, county jailers, and emergency telecommunications operators. Potential officers and jailers are required to take a licensing examination

The commission also regulates minimum requirements for police officer pre-service and in-service training. TCLEOSE mandates a minimum of 540 hours of training for police officer candidates, although individual departments are free to require a longer period of training. After pre-service training is successfully completed, all candidates must pass a state licensing examination, which is developed and administered by the Commission. The examination consists of 150 multiple choice questions which reflect the learning objectives of the basic academy training. Candidates passing this examination receive a peace officer license. Jailer candidates are also required to pass a similar examination.

In-service training or education is that in which an individual receives after employment and performing the duties of that position. In police work, in-service training is conducted after the individual has some policing experience and continues throughout the officer's career. The purpose of in-service training is to ensure that all officers are kept informed of current legislative statutes, department regulations, and community expectations of the organization.

According to §217.9 of the Texas Administrative Code, all police officers are required to attend a minimum of 40 hours of in-service training every two years, although agencies are not limited to this minimum number of hours of continuing education and most officers in Texas receive more than the minimum required amount of training. Today, many in-service classes are offered over the Internet.

Mandatory topics required of all officers include:

- training in civil rights, racial sensitivity, and cultural diversity
- training in recognition and documentation of cases involving child abuse, child neglect, family violence, sexual assault, and issues concerning sex offender characteristics

Other requirements are specified by the Code for constables, deputy constables, and supervisory peace officers. An officer who fails to complete the required in-service/continuing education training may have his/her peace officer's license suspended by the Commission.

CHAPTER 5

THE COURT SYSTEM IN TEXAS

Schmalleger (see pp.292-306) discusses the general outline of the criminal courts in the United States at both the federal and state levels. The Texas court system, which includes the criminal courts, is somewhat more complex than the court system found in most other states. Texas has a five-level court structure, with two top-level appellate courts, an intermediate appellate court, state trial courts of general jurisdiction, county trial courts of limited jurisdiction, and local trial courts of limited jurisdiction.

UNITED STATES FEDERAL COURTS

Although they are not specifically part of the Texas state court system, there are four **U.S. District Courts** (see Schmalleger, p.301-302) which sit in Texas. These are the trial courts of the federal system. These courts include:

1. The Texas Southern District Court, which is headquartered in Houston and has 18 authorized judgeships

2. The Texas Northern District Court, which is headquartered in Dallas and has 12 authorized judgeships

3. The Texas Western District Court, which is headquartered in San Antonio and has 12 authorized judgeships

4. The Texas Eastern District Court, which is headquartered in Tyler and has 14 authorized judgeships.

The **U.S. Courts of Appeals** (see Schmalleger, pp.302-303) are the intermediate appellate courts of the federal court system and have appellate jurisdiction only over federal laws. Judges in these courts are nominated by the President of the United States and confirmed by the Senate. Texas, along with Louisiana and Mississippi, is part of the Fifth Circuit, which sits in New Orleans, LA. The U.S. Courts of Appeals are not to be confused with the Texas Courts of Appeals.

THE BASIC COURT STRUCTURE OF TEXAS

The court structure of Texas is a five-tier structure. Rather than one "court of last resort," Texas has two: the Texas Supreme Court and the Texas Court of Criminal Appeals. These courts are of equal rank but have different jurisdictions; they serve as the highest appellate courts in the state.

The second level includes the Courts of Appeals, which serve as the intermediate appellate courts for the state of Texas.

The third level of the court structure is composed of state trial courts of general jurisdiction. In Texas, these are known as District Courts (and are not to be confused with the U.S. District Courts discussed above).

The fourth tier includes county trial courts of limited jurisdiction. All counties have a Constitutional County Court. In addition, some counties also have County Courts at Law and/or Statutory Probate Courts. These courts are of equal rank but differ in their jurisdictions.

Finally, the fifth tier includes local trial courts of limited jurisdiction. These include Municipal Courts and Justice of the Peace Courts.

Not all of these courts have criminal jurisdiction. According to Section 4.01 of the Code of Criminal Procedure (CCrP):

> The following courts have jurisdiction in criminal actions:
> 1. The Court of Criminal Appeals;
> 2. Courts of appeals;
> 3. The district courts;
> 4. The criminal district courts;
> 5. The magistrates appointed by the judges of the district courts of Bexar County, Dallas County, Tarrant County, or Travis County that give preference to criminal cases and the magistrates appointed by the judges of the criminal district courts of Dallas County or Tarrant County;
> 6. The county courts;
> 7. All county courts at law with criminal jurisdiction;
> 8. County criminal courts;
> 9. Justice courts;
> 10. Municipal courts; and
> 11. The magistrates appointed by the judges of the district courts of Lubbock County.

TEXAS' HIGHEST APPELLATE COURTS

Schmalleger (see p.297) discusses state appellate courts. As noted above, Texas has two high-level appellate courts authorized to hear final appeals.

The Supreme Court of Texas

The **Texas Supreme Court** has final appellate jurisdiction in all civil and juvenile cases throughout Texas. Most cases are on appeal from an intermediate Court of Appeal. The court has a total of nine justices, including a Chief Justice. Five justices constitute a quorum and the concurrence of at least five of the nine justices is required to decide a case. To serve as a Supreme Court justice, an individual must be at least 35 years of age, be a citizen of the U.S. and of Texas, be licensed to practice law in Texas, and have been a practicing lawyer, or lawyer and a lawyer and judge of a court of record, for at least ten years. Justices are elected to six-year terms at a general election. The Texas Supreme Court has no criminal jurisdiction.

The Court of Criminal Appeals

The **Court of Criminal Appeals** has final appellate jurisdiction in the state over all appeals that result from criminal cases. Most cases are appeals from an intermediate Court of Appeal; cases may be appealed by petition for discretionary review which can be filed by the state and/or the defendant. In addition, all cases that involve a sentence of death are automatically appealed directly to the Court of Criminal Appeals from the trial court level. The court also has the right to review any decision on its own motion. The court sits in Austin.

The jurisdiction of the Court of Criminal Appeals is outlined in CCrP §4.04, which states that:

> 1. The Court of Criminal Appeals and each judge thereof shall have, and is hereby given, the power and authority to grant and issue and cause the issuance of writs of habeas corpus, and, in criminal law matters, the writs of mandamus, procedendo, prohibition, and certiorari. The court and each judge thereof shall have, and is hereby given, the power and authority to grant and issue and cause the issuance of such other writs as may be necessary to protect its jurisdiction or enforce its judgments.
>
> 2. The Court of Criminal Appeals shall have, and is hereby given, final appellate and review jurisdiction in criminal cases coextensive with the limits of the state, and its determinations shall be final. The appeal of all cases in which the death penalty has been assessed shall be to the Court of Criminal Appeals. In addition, the Court of Criminal Appeals may, on its own motion, with or without a petition for such discretionary review being filed by one of the parties, review any decision of a court of appeals in a criminal case. Discretionary review by the Court of Criminal Appeals is not a matter of right, but of sound judicial discretion.

The Court of Criminal Appeals is composed of nine judges, one of whom serves as the Presiding Judge. The qualifications needed to serve as a judge in the Court of Criminal Appeals are the same as those required for Supreme Court Justices; judges also receive the same salaries as their counterparts in the Supreme Court. All judges are elected to six-year terms. The court may sit in panels of three judges to hear cases; in a three-judge panel, two judges constitute a quorum and the agreement of two judges is required for a decision. For any proceedings involving capital punishment, the full court must convene; in these situations, five judges constitute a quorum and the agreement of five judges is required for a decision.

TEXAS COURTS OF APPEALS

The intermediate appellate courts in Texas are known as **Courts of Appeals** (see Schmalleger, p.297). The state is divided into fourteen appellate districts, each with a Court of Appeals. The composition of each district is outlined in Section 22.201 of the Government Code (GC). These courts have intermediate appellate jurisdiction within their districts in both civil and criminal cases that have been appealed from either district courts or county-level courts, except for those cases which involved a sentence of death.

Each Court of Appeals has a Chief Justice and at least two but not more than twelve additional justices. All justices must meet the same qualifications required of Supreme Court justices and Court of Criminal Appeals judges. The exact number of judges assigned to each Court of Appeals is determined by statute and listed in GC §22.216. The largest is the Court of Appeals for the Fifth District, which consists of a chief justice and twelve justices. This district is composed of seven counties: Collin, Dallas, Grayson, Hunt, Kaufman, Rockwall, and Van Zandt; the court sits primarily in the City of Dallas. Currently, there are a total of 80 justices authorized to sit in the Courts of Appeals. Most appeals in these courts are heard by a panel of three judges, with the agreement of a majority of the judges sitting required to decide a case.

TEXAS DISTRICT COURTS

Texas District Courts serve as the state's trial courts of general jurisdiction (see Schmalleger, p.296-297). The state is divided into judicial districts, each of which has a district court with one or more judges. District judges are elected to four-year terms. To qualify as a district judge, an individual must be a citizen of the United States and of Texas, must be at least 25 years of age, must be licensed to practice law in Texas, must have been a practicing lawyer or judge of a court in Texas for at least four years prior to election, and must have resided in the district from which he/she is elected for at least two years preceding election. All district court judges must live in their districts during their terms of office.

The area served by each district is established by the state legislature. However, each county must have at least one district court. In areas with very low populations, one district may include several counties, all of which are served by one district court. On the other hand, highly populous urban counties may be divided up among several districts and be served by a number of different district courts.

The jurisdiction of the district court is outlined in Article V, Section 8, of the Texas Constitution, which states that:

> District Court jurisdiction consists of exclusive, appellate, and original jurisdiction of all actions, proceedings, and remedies, except in cases where exclusive, appellate, or original jurisdiction may be conferred by this Constitution or other law on some other court, tribunal, or administrative body. District Court judges shall have the power to issue writs necessary to enforce their jurisdiction. The District Court shall have appellate jurisdiction and general supervisory control over the County Commissioners Court, with such exceptions and under such regulations as may be prescribed by law.

Essentially, District Courts have original jurisdiction over all felony criminal cases, all civil cases involving at least $200, all divorce cases, and various other matters. Most district courts handle both civil and criminal cases but some courts, located in more highly-populated counties, may specialize in criminal, civil, family law, or juvenile cases.

COUNTY TRIAL COURTS OF LIMITED JURISDICTION

The fourth level of courts in Texas are the **County Trial Courts of Limited Jurisdiction**. There are three different types of county courts: Constitutional County Courts, County Courts at Law, and Statutory Probate Courts (see Schmalleger, p.296, for a brief discussion of lower courts).

Constitutional County Courts

According to Article 5, Section 15, of the Texas Constitution, each of the 254 counties Texas is required to have a **Constitutional County Court**. The presiding officer of the court, the county judge, is elected by voters in the county to a four-year term. Article 5, Section 15, of the Constitution states that, to be a county judge, an individual must be "well informed in the law of the State [and] a conservator of the peace..." Each county is specifically limited to only one county court.

Constitutional County Courts have limited civil and criminal jurisdiction. They generally hear probate cases filed in the county (unless the county has a Statutory Probate Court), have original jurisdiction over all Class A and Class B misdemeanor cases, and, in those counties which have not established County Courts at Law, have appellate jurisdiction over those cases which are appealed from municipal courts or justice of the peace courts. Unless the appeal is being made from a municipal court of record, the appeal consists of a completely new trial (a ***trial de novo***).

County Courts at Law

Because each county is constitutionally limited to only one county court, some larger counties also have **County Courts at Law** which are intended to assist the county court. The jurisdiction of these courts varies by county and is determined by the statute that created each specific court. In most counties, these courts (not the Constitutional County Court) have appellate jurisdiction over cases appealed from justice of the peace or municipal courts.

According to CCrP §25.0014, to qualify as a judge of a statutory county court (such as a County Court at Law), an individual must:

> (1) be at least 25 years of age;
> (2) have resided in the county for at least two years before election or appointment; and
> (3) be a licensed attorney in this state who has practiced law or served as a judge of a court in this state, or both combined, for the four years preceding election or appointment, unless otherwise provided for by law.

Statutory Probate Courts

Although in most counties, the Constitutional County Court has original probate jurisdiction, in some counties the legislature authorized the creation of **Statutory Probate Courts** which share this original jurisdiction. Thus, the Statutory Probate Court and the Constitutional County Court will have concurrent jurisdiction over probate matters. Each of the six largest metropolitan areas in the state have Statutory Probate Courts, which have original jurisdiction over probate matters, guardianship issues, and mental health commitments within the county.

LOCAL TRIAL COURTS OF LIMITED JURISDICTION

The fifth and lowest level of courts in Texas are the **Local Trial Courts of Limited Jurisdiction**. There are two main types of local trial courts: Municipal Courts and Justice of the Peace Courts (see Schmalleger, p.294).

Municipal Courts

According to CCrP §29.002, each municipality in Texas has a **Municipal Court**. There are approximately 850 incorporated cities and towns in the state, each of which has at least one such court; the larger cities may have multiple municipal courts, depending on the city's population and needs.

The jurisdiction of the Municipal Court is outlined in CCrP §29.003, which states that:

> (a) A municipal court, including a municipal court of record, shall have exclusive original jurisdiction within the municipality's territorial limits and property owned by the municipality located in the municipality's extraterritorial jurisdiction in all criminal cases that:
> (1) arise under:
> (A) the ordinances of the municipality; or
> (B) a resolution, rule, or order of a joint board operating an airport under Section 22.074, Transportation Code; and
> (2) are punishable by a fine not to exceed:
> (A) $2,000 in all cases arising under municipal ordinances or resolutions, rules, or orders of a joint board that govern fire safety, zoning, or public health and sanitation, including dumping of refuse; or
> (B) $500 in all other cases arising under a municipal ordinance or a resolution, rule, or order of a joint board.
> (b) The municipal court has concurrent jurisdiction with the justice court of a precinct in which the municipality is located in all criminal cases arising under state law that:
> (1) arise within the municipality's territorial limits or property owned by the municipality located in the municipality's extraterritorial

jurisdiction and are punishable only by a fine, as defined in Subsection (c); or

(2) arise under Chapter 106, Alcoholic Beverage Code, and do not include confinement as an authorized sanction.

(c) In this section, an offense which is punishable by "fine only" is defined as an offense that is punishable by fine and such sanctions, if any, as authorized by statute not consisting of confinement in jail or imprisonment.

(d) The fact that a conviction in a municipal court has as a consequence the imposition of a penalty or sanction by an agency or entity other than the court, such as a denial, suspension, or revocation of a privilege, does not affect the original jurisdiction of the municipal court.

(e) The municipal court has jurisdiction in the forfeiture and final judgment of all bail bonds and personal bonds taken in criminal cases of which the court has jurisdiction.

Essentially, municipal courts have original jurisdiction over all violations of city ordinances and have concurrent jurisdiction with justice of the peace courts over any Class C misdemeanors which are punishable only by a fine. They generally do not have jurisdiction in civil cases, with the exception of cases involving owners of dangerous dogs. Municipal judges have the power to issue search warrants and arrest warrants.

Justice of the Peace Courts

Each county is required by constitution to establish between one and eight justice of the peace precincts. The actual number of precincts in each county is determined by the county population. Each precinct has either one or two **Justice of the Peace Courts**, depending on the population of the precinct. Currently, there are approximately 900 justice of the peace courts in the state. Justices of the peace are elected by the voters of the precinct to four-year terms.

Justice of the peace courts have original jurisdiction over minor civil cases and over Class C misdemeanor criminal cases. They also serve as a small claims court. Justices of the peace have the power to issue search warrants and arrest warrants; in some counties, they also serve as the county coroner if the county does not provide for a medical examiner.

OTHER COURT AGENCIES AND COMMISSIONS

The Texas Office of Court Administration

The **Texas Office of Court Administration** (OCA) provides technical assistance and administrative support to courts throughout the state (see Schmalleger, pp. 299-300). It is under the direction of the chief justice of the state supreme court.

The duties and responsibilities of the OCA include providing software to assist the courts in tracking caseloads and automating reports; providing technical support to courts; and supplying information on recent developments and court trends to the legislature, the courts, and members of the general public. The OCA is also responsible for gathering official statistics from court officials throughout the state.

The State Commission on Judicial Conduct

The **State Commission on Judicial Conduct** was created in 1965 by the passage of Article 5, Section 1-a, of the Texas Constitution and is responsible for reviewing all complaints regarding misconduct or disability of judges and justices in Texas. The commission has jurisdiction over all judicial officers in the state. Currently, there are approximately 3,000 judicial officers under the jurisdiction of the commission.

After receiving a complaint about a judge or justice, the commission investigates and then holds a hearing. If the commission determines that the judge or justice is guilty of some type of misconduct that is inconsistent with the proper performance of his or her duties, the commission may:

- privately reprimand the judge
- publicly censure the judge
- recommend to the Texas Supreme Court that the judge be removed or retired.

The State Bar of Texas and the Texas Bar Association

In 1939, the state legislature passed the **State Bar Act**, which required all attorneys who are licenced to practice law in Texas to be members of the State Bar. The **State Bar of Texas** is an administrative agency under the authority of the judicial branch of the state government. It is a public corporation funded by attorney dues and Professional Development Program Fees and is responsible for providing educational programs for the legal profession and the public, administering the Minimum Continuing Legal Education program for attorneys, and managing the lawyer disciplinary process.

TEXAS CRIMINAL COURT PROCEDURES

Schmalleger (see pp.16-20, pp.306-314, and pp.339-353) outlines the basic procedures involved in a criminal trial. The specific procedures used in the Texas criminal court system are similar to those discussed in Schmalleger. The criminal case begins when a person is arrested, a prosecutor files formal charges, or a grand jury issues an indictment. Before being brought before a judge, the arrested individual is booked and the prosecutor consults with the arresting officer. If the prosecutor decides there is sufficient evidence, he/she will prepare the charges against the defendant.

Initial Appearance

Within 24 hours of arrest, the defendant must be brought before a judge for an **initial appearance** (see Schmalleger, p.18 and pp.306-307). At this time, the judge will inform the defendant of the charges being brought against him/her and will determine whether the defendant is entitled to any form of pretrial release, and if so, which type (see Schmalleger, pp.307-310). In some cases, the judge may set bail; in other cases the defendants may request to be released on their own recognizance, without having to pay bail, or may be placed in the custody and under the supervision of a specific individual or agency.

The prosecution may charge the defendant either by an **information** or by a **grand jury indictment** (see Schmalleger, p.19). Both are formal charging instruments which specify the accused individual, the specific crime, and the court which has jurisdiction to try the case. An information is defined in CCrP §21.20 as:

> a written statement filed and presented in behalf of the State by the district or county attorney, charging the defendant with an offense which may by law be so prosecuted.

A grand jury indictment is defined by CCrP §21.01 as

> the written statement of a grand jury accusing a person therein named of some act or omission which, by law, is declared to be an offense.

Grand juries (see Schmalleger, p.19 and p.311) are organized by the district judge and have jurisdiction only over those crimes occurring within the county. They generally have 12 jurors. The grand jury does not determine the defendant's guilt or innocence; its purpose is simply to determine whether or not there is sufficient evidence to charge the individual with a crime. For an indictment or **true bill** to be issued, at least nine of the twelve grand jurors must agree. If the grand jury does not find that there is sufficient evidence to charge the suspect, the case is **no billed** and the suspect is immediately discharged. A finding of no bill does not bar this or any other grand jury from indicting the same suspect at a later data. Capital felonies may only be charged by indictment.

Arraignment

The next stage in the criminal process is the **arraignment** (see Schmalleger, p.19 and p.312). According to CCrP §26.01:

> In all felony cases, after indictment, and all misdemeanor cases punishable by imprisonment, there shall be an arraignment.

At this time, the defendant is asked to plead to the charges. He/she may plead guilty, not guilty, or *nolo contendere*, although not all judges permit a plea of *nolo contendere*. Generally defendants will plead either guilty or not guilty.

If the accused pleads guilty (or *nolo contendere*), there is no need for the case to go to trial and the offender will be sentenced.

If the defendant has been charged with a felony or a misdemeanor that is punishable by imprisonment and cannot afford to hire an attorney, the court at this time will appoint an attorney to represent the defendant (see Schmalleger, pp.328-330). Court-appointed attorneys are not appointed for indigent defendants in cases where the defendant is charged with a crime that will not result in a possible term of imprisonment.

Plea Bargaining

Schmalleger (see pp.312-314) discusses the issue of plea bargaining in detail. While plea bargaining is not a formal stage of the criminal justice process, it is an extremely important process in every state, including Texas. Most criminal cases in Texas are resolved by plea bargaining; very few cases actually go to trial. Generally, plea bargaining involves an attempt to resolve or dispose of a case without a trial, by an agreement between the prosecutor and the defendant, made under judicial supervision.

There are a variety of possible plea bargains. In some cases, the defendant agrees to plead guilty in exchange for the prosecutor's promise to recommend to the judge that a particular sentence be imposed. If the judge rejects the agreement, the defendant has the right to withdraw his or her plea of guilty. Another type of plea bargain occurs when the prosecutor allows the defendant to plead guilty to a less serious offense than the one with which the defendant was originally charged. This type of plea bargain reduces the range of possible sentences that the judge may impose.

All plea bargains must be approved by the judge. Plea bargaining often begins at the arraignment stage but may continue up to and even during the trial.

Pre-Trial Motions

Prior to the trial, both the defense and the prosecution have the opportunity to make a variety of **pre-trial motions** (see Schmalleger, pp.347-348). A **motion for continuance** is a request that the trial be delayed for a period of time; this may be made by either the prosecution or the defense. A **motion to suppress evidence** considers whether evidence to be presented at trial was obtained illegally (e.g., through an unlawful search and seizure) and should therefore be prohibited for use as evidence in court. A **motion for a change of venue** may be filed by either the prosecution or the defendant. This motion requests that the location of the trial be changed on the grounds that it is not possible to obtain a fair and impartial trial in the county where the case is currently pending. A **motion to dismiss** is filed by the defense and claims that there are no grounds for bringing the defendant to trial.

The Right to a Speedy Trial

Schmalleger (see pp.341-342) discusses the constitutional right to a **speedy trial**. The Texas Constitution also provides for a speedy trial (Article I, Section 10). In Texas, each case must be brought to trial within a certain specified period of time, which is outlined in CCrP 32A.02, Section 1:

> A court shall grant a motion to set aside an indictment, information, or complaint if the state is not ready for trial within:
> (1) 180 days of the commencement of a criminal action if the defendant is accused of a felony;
> (2) 90 days of the commencement of a criminal action if the defendant is accused of a misdemeanor punishable by a sentence of imprisonment for more than 180 days; or

(3) 60 days of the commencement of a criminal action if the defendant is accused of a misdemeanor punishable by a sentence of imprisonment for 180 days or less or punishable by a fine only.

However, if the defendant is responsible for delays in bringing the case to trial, these delay periods are not included in the specified maximum pre-trial period. If the prosecutor is not ready to try the case within the legally specified period, and the defendant is not responsible for the delay, the judge, upon a defense motion, must dismiss the case.

The Trial

Less than ten percent of all felony and misdemeanor cases go to a formal criminal **trial** (see Schmalleger, pp.19-20); the vast majority are disposed of by a plea of guilty on the part of the defendant. If the defendant enters a plea of not guilty and the case does go to trial, the procedure is similar regardless of the seriousness of the charge against the defendant.

All defendants are constitutionally guaranteed the right to a **trial by jury**. However, with the consent of the judge and the prosecutor, a defendant may waive the right to a jury trial and be tried in front of a judge. This is known as a **bench trial** (see Schmalleger, p.20). A defendant charged with a capital felony in which the state plans to seek the death penalty may not waive his/her right to a trial by jury.

Jury Selection

The first step in a trial is the selection of the jury. District court juries are composed of twelve jurors; county courts and justice of the peace courts use six-person juries.

Schmalleger (see pp.342-345) discusses the topic of jury selection in detail. As noted in Schmalleger (see p.342), the process of jury selection is known as ***voir dire*** and involves an examination of the prospective jurors by the attorneys for both the prosecution and the defense, and sometimes by the judge as well. The main purpose of the *voir dire* is to determine whether the potential juror can be fair and impartial. During the process, both the defense and the district attorneys are allowed to make challenges, or to object to the inclusion of certain potential trial jurors. Two types of challenges are allowed. A **challenge for cause** (see Schmalleger p.342) is made when the attorney feels that the juror is either unfit or incapable of serving on the jury. According to CCrP §35.16(a), challenges for cause may be made by either the prosecution or the defense for any of the following reasons:

1. That he is not a qualified voter in the state and county under the Constitution and laws of the state; provided, however, the failure to register to vote shall not be a disqualification;
2. That he has been convicted of theft or any felony;
3. That he is under indictment or other legal accusation for theft or any felony;
4. That he is insane;
5. That he has such defect in the organs of feeling or hearing, or such bodily or mental defect or disease as to render him unfit for jury service, or that he is legally blind and the court in its discretion is not satisfied that he is fit for jury service in that particular case;
6. That he is a witness in the case;

7. That he served on the grand jury which found the indictment;
8. That he served on a petit jury in a former trial of the same case;
9. That he has a bias or prejudice in favor of or against the defendant;
10. That from hearsay, or otherwise, there is established in the mind of the juror such a conclusion as to the guilt or innocence of the defendant as would influence him in his action in finding a verdict. To ascertain whether this cause of challenge exists, the juror shall first be asked whether, in his opinion, the conclusion so established will influence his verdict. If he answers in the affirmative, he shall be discharged without further interrogation by either party or the court. If he answers in the negative, he shall be further examined as to how his conclusion was formed, and the extent to which it will affect his action; and, if it appears to have been formed from reading newspaper accounts, communications, statements or reports or mere rumor or hearsay, and if the juror states that he feels able, notwithstanding such opinion, to render an impartial verdict upon the law and the evidence, the court, if satisfied that he is impartial and will render such verdict, may, in its discretion, admit him as competent to serve in such case. If the court, in its discretion, is not satisfied that he is impartial, the juror shall be discharged;
11. That he cannot read or write...

According to CCrP §35.16(b), the state only may make challenges for cause for any of the following reasons:

1. That the juror has conscientious scruples in regard to the infliction of the punishment of death for crime, in a capital case, where the State is seeking the death penalty;
2. That he is related within the third degree of consanguinity or affinity, as determined under Chapter 573, Government Code, to the defendant; and
3. That he has a bias or prejudice against any phase of the law upon which the State is entitled to rely for conviction or punishment.

In addition, according to CCrP §35.16(c), the defense may make challenges for cause on the following grounds:

1. That he is related within the third degree of consanguinity or affinity, as determined under Chapter 573, Government Code, to the person injured by the commission of the offense, or to any prosecutor in the case; and
2. That he has a bias or prejudice against any of the law applicable to the case upon which the defense is entitled to rely, either as a defense to some phase of the offense for which the defendant is being prosecuted or as a mitigation thereof or of the punishment therefor.

Peremptory challenges (see Schmalleger, p.342 and p.346) may be used by either attorney to remove potential jurors from the jury panel without giving any reasons. In capital cases where the death penalty is being sought, both the defense and the prosecution are allowed fifteen peremptory challenges. In non-capital felony cases and in capital cases where the death penalty is not being sought, each side is allowed ten peremptory challenges. In misdemeanor cases tried in district court, five peremptory challenges are allowed; if the case is being tried in the county court or county court at law, three are permitted. CCrP §35.261 prohibits peremptory challenges based on the race of the potential juror (see Schmalleger, pp.343-344 and p.346 for a discussion of jury selection and race).

After the selection of the jury is completed, the jurors are sworn in by the court and seated in the jury box (see Schmalleger, p.345). CCrP §35.22 gives the oath of trial jurors:

> "You and each of you do solemnly swear that in the case of the State of Texas against the defendant, you will a true verdict render according to the law and the evidence, so help you God".

The information or indictment is read to the jury by the prosecutor and the defendant enters a plea before the court.

Opening Statements

Schmalleger (see p.345 and p.349) discusses the use of **opening statements**. Both the prosecutor and the defense attorney are entitled to make an opening statement which provides all the participants in the trial, especially the jury, with an overview of the facts of the case. In Texas, the prosecutor makes the first statement.

Presentation of the Prosecution's Evidence

After the opening statements are completed, the prosecution begins to present evidence in support of the charge that has been brought against the defendant. The prosecution presents first because the state is bringing the charge against the defendant and, because of the presumption of innocence, has assumed the burden of proof. In Texas, evidence submitted into court may include the sworn testimony of witnesses as well as exhibits such as pictures, documents, or other objects (see Schmalleger, pp.349-352 for a discussion of various types of evidence).

The prosecutor generally begins with the **direct examination** of the prosecution's first witness, who is obviously expected to give evidence to support the state's case against the defendant. After the prosecutor finishes questioning the witness, the defense is allowed to **cross-examine** the same witness. If the prosecutor wishes, he/she may then return to ask the witness more questions in a process that is known as **re-direct examination**. Following this, the defense attorney has the option to question the witness once more during the **re-cross examination**. This procedure is repeated for each witness called by the prosecution.

Presentation of the Defense's Evidence

After the prosecution has presented all its evidence and called all its witnesses, the defense may then offer evidence. Although the prosecution is required to present evidence in support of the indictment, the presentation of evidence in defense of the defendant is optional. The procedure for the presentation of the evidence by the defense is similar to that of the prosecution: direct examination, cross examination, re-direct, and re-cross. The defendant is not required to testify at any point in the trial; both the U.S. Constitution and the Texas Constitution protect the defendant against self-incrimination (see Schmalleger, p.349)

Rebuttal and Surrebuttal

After the defense has presented its evidence, the prosecution is entitled to present a **rebuttal** case. At this time, the prosecutor may present evidence in response to the case presented by the defense. The defense may also be entitled to present a **surrebuttal** case, which involves presenting evidence after the prosecution has completed the rebuttal. However, this is at the discretion of the trial court.

Closing Arguments

Once all the evidence is presented, each side is given the opportunity to make a **closing argument** or **summation** (see Schmalleger, pp.352-353). In the closing arguments, each attorney reviews and summarizes the evidence that best supports his/her side of case, discusses any inferences that may be drawn from that evidence, and points out weaknesses in the opponent's case. In Texas, the defense presents closing arguments first, with the goal of trying to persuade the jury to acquit the defendant. When the defense has completed its closing arguments, the prosecution has the right to make the concluding address to the jury, to try to persuade the jury to convict the defendant. Closing arguments are optional for both the prosecution and defense.

Charging the Jury

After the closing arguments are completed, the judge has the opportunity to provide instructions to the jury regarding any legal issues or points of law which are applicable to the case. This step is known as **charging the jury** or as **jury instruction** (see Schmalleger, p.353). The judge may not sum up the evidence or make comments on the credibility of witnesses or the guilt of the defendant; he/she may only instruct the jury as to what law or laws must be applied to the evidence of the specific case.

Jury Deliberation and Verdict Rendition

After the judge has given instructions to the jury, the jury retires to the jury room for **deliberation** (see Schmalleger, p.353). At this time, the jurors discuss the case and attempt to come to agreement on a verdict concerning the guilt or innocence of the defendant. Texas requires that all the jurors unanimously agree on a guilty verdict before the defendant can be convicted of a crime. If the jurors are unable to agree on a verdict after a reasonable period of time, they are considered to be a "**hung jury**." If this happens, the judge will declare a **mistrial** and the case may have to be retried in front of a new jury.

If the jurors come to an agreement on a **verdict**, they are returned to the courtroom by the bailiff and the verdict is read in open court. After the verdict is rendered, the jurors must be collectively asked whether this is their verdict. In addition, either the defense or the prosecution is entitled to request a poll of the individual members of the jury to ensure that each member of the jury agrees with the verdict and that no member was coerced or intimidated into agreeing, or agreed simply out of exhaustion. If in either the collective or individual poll, any juror responds negatively, the court must refuse to accept the verdict and direct the jury to resume deliberations.

If the verdict of the jury is not guilty, the trial is over and the defendant must be immediately discharged from custody and is entitled to the return of any bail money and the exoneration of any sureties. The trial court judge is required to accept a verdict of not guilty. Because of the state and federal constitutional protections against double jeopardy, the defendant may never be tried in state court for those same charges.

Proceedings Between the Verdict and the Sentence

If the defendant is found guilty, he/she will be sentenced. However, after a verdict of guilty is rendered and before the sentencing phase of the trial, the defendant may make a **post-trial motion** (see Schmalleger, pp.347-348) to set aside or modify the verdict. If the judge sets aside the verdict, the defendant may be entitled to a dismissal, a reduction of the charges, or a new trial. These motions are rarely granted.

The Sentence

If the defendant is found guilty, he/she will be sentenced by a judge. In most cases, the trial judge will pronounce the sentence, although in some situations it may be necessary for sentence to be pronounced by a different judge. See Schmalleger (p.20) for a brief overview of sentencing and Chapter 10 of Schmalleger for a more in-depth discussion. The sentencing process is discussed in more detail in the next chapter of this supplement.

Appeals

If the defendant is convicted of a crime, he/she may have the option of **appealing** the conviction (see Schmalleger, p.297). In most cases, an appeal does not involve retrying a case or re-examining the factual issues surrounding the crime; it only involves an examination or review of the legal issues involved in the case. The purpose of an appeal is to make certain that the defendant received a fair trial, that he/she was not deprived of any constitutional rights at any time, and that no errors were committed at the trial that require an **acquittal** or a **retrial**. In most cases, if a defendant wins on appeal, he/she will be retried; in some cases (although this is fairly rare), the case may be reversed and the defendant acquitted. In general, the defendant has the right to appeal regardless of:

- the crime of which he/she was convicted;
- the sentence received; and
- whether he/she was convicted after a trial or by a plea of guilty.

In some cases, the defendant may be asked to give up his or her right to appeal as a part of the plea bargain. However, even if this is the case, the defendant may be permitted to have the appellate court review certain issues regarding the case.

CHAPTER 6

SENTENCING IN TEXAS

INTRODUCTION

After a criminal defendant pleads guilty or is found guilty in court by a judge or jury, the judge must impose a sentence of punishment upon the offender. CCrP §42.02 defines a **sentence** as

> that part of the judgment, or order revoking a suspension of the imposition of a sentence, that orders that the punishment be carried into execution in the manner prescribed by law.

In a felony case, the sentence must be pronounced in open court, in the presence of the defendant, although in a misdemeanor case, the judgment and sentence may be pronounced in the defendant's absence. Schmalleger (see pp.365-369) outlines the general philosophy of criminal sentencing, including the justifications and aims of punishment.

In every case in which a conviction has been entered, the court is required to pronounce sentence. If the defendant has been found guilty on multiple counts, the court must pronounce sentence on each count. In all cases, the judge determines the final sentence

TYPES OF SENTENCES

A variety of sentences may be imposed upon convicted offenders in Texas (see Schmalleger, p.386). Sentences acceptable in the Texas courts include:

- fines
- community service
- restitution
- probation
- other community-based or intermediate sanctions (e.g., boot camp, house arrest with electronic monitoring, shock incarceration)
- incarceration in a jail or prison
- death

Combinations of these sentences are also allowed. For example, a judge may order both imprisonment and a fine, or order the offender to pay a fine as well as victim restitution. However, the judge has only a limited amount of discretion when imposing a sentence; he/she must follow the authorized punishments outlined in Chapter 12 of the Texas Penal Code.

THE PRESENTENCE REPORT

After a defendant is found guilty of a crime (either by pleading guilty at arraignment or by conviction at trial), he/she will be sentenced by the court. In most cases, the judge will order the preparation of a **presentence report** (see Schmalleger, pp.379-381). This report contains information about the offender's background and about the circumstances of the crime.

According to CCrP §42.12, Sec.9(b), the judge is not required to order a presentence report in a misdemeanor case if:

(1) the defendant requests that a report not be made and the judge agrees to the request; or
(2) the judge finds that there is sufficient information in the record to permit the meaningful exercise of sentencing discretion and the judge explains this finding on the record.

According to CCrP §42.12, Sec.9(g), if the defendant is being sentenced for a felony, a presentence report does not have to be prepared (unless the defendant requests one) if:

(1) punishment is to be assessed by a jury;
(2) the defendant is convicted of or enters a plea of guilty or nolo contendere to capital murder;
(3) the only available punishment is imprisonment; or
(4) the judge is informed that a plea bargain agreement exists, under which the defendant agrees to a punishment of imprisonment, and the judge intends to follow the agreement.

In all other cases, a presentence report must be prepared prior to sentencing. CCrP §42.12, Sec.9(a) outlines the main contents of such a report, which include:

> ...the circumstances of the offense with which the defendant is charged, the amount of restitution necessary to adequately compensate a victim of the offense, the criminal and social history of the defendant, and any other information relating to the defendant or the offense requested by the judge. It is not necessary that the report contain a sentencing recommendation, but the report must contain a proposed client supervision plan describing programs and sanctions that the community supervision and corrections department would provide the defendant if the judge suspended the imposition of the sentence or granted deferred adjudication.

Prior to sentencing, the defendant and/or his/her counsel have the right to read the report and to comment upon it.

DETERMINATE AND INDETERMINATE SENTENCING

Schmalleger (see pp.371-374) discusses the concept of **structured** or **determinate sentencing**. A determinate sentence is a flat or fixed-term prison sentence for an offense. In other words, rather than passing a sentence that includes a range of time to be served in prison (for example, three to five years in the state prison), the sentence is a fixed period of time (for example, four years in prison). A sentence that includes a range of time between a specified minimum and maximum is known as an **indeterminate sentence** (see Schmalleger, pp.369-371).

In Texas, all offenders sentenced to a term of imprisonment receive a determinate sentence. Thus, although, for example, the statutory sentence of imprisonment for a second degree felony is a term of not less than two years nor more than 20 years, the court must sentence the offender to a specific fixed period of time within that range. The judge may not sentence the offender to, for example, a sentence of four to six years.

CONCURRENT VERSUS CONSECUTIVE SENTENCES

If an offender is convicted of multiple offenses, the court may impose a sentence for each offense. If the sentences imposed involve terms of imprisonment the court has the option of requiring the sentences to be served concurrently or consecutively. **Concurrent sentences** are served at the same time. **Consecutive sentences** or **cumulative sentences** are served in succession, one after the other (see Schmalleger, p.20).

In most situations, the court has the discretion to determine whether multiple sentences will be served concurrently or consecutively. However, in some circumstances, the law sets forth specific requirements and removes the discretion from the court.

For example, CCRP §42.08(b) states that:

> If a defendant is sentenced for an offense committed while the defendant was an inmate in the institutional division of the Texas Department of Criminal Justice and the defendant has not completed the sentence he was serving at the time of the offense, the judge shall order the sentence for the subsequent offense to commence immediately on completion of the sentence for the original offense.

Thus, in this situation, the sentences for the new crime and the old crime must be served consecutively, rather than concurrently.

SENTENCES OF IMPRISONMENT

According to the Texas Penal Code, crimes are classified into categories which are based on the relative seriousness of the offense. Each category of crimes has an associated punishment

Felony Offenses

Felonies in Texas are classified into five categories, which are listed in Pen §12.04. The associated punishments for these crimes are defined in Pen §12.31 through Pen §12.35.

A **capital felony** is the most serious category of crime in Texas. A crime falling into this category is punishable either by death or by imprisonment for life in a state institution. The only death penalty offense that has ever existed in Texas is the crime of capital murder. In a capital case, the state is required to state prior to trial whether or not they plan to seek the death penalty as punishment for the crime; this information must also be provided to prospective jury members.

A **first degree felony** is punishable by life imprisonment, or by a term of not less than five years nor more than 99 years. Murder, other than capital murder, is a first degree felony in Texas. Aggravated sexual assault and aggravated robbery are other examples of first degree felonies. In total, there are over 30 first degree felonies in Texas.

A **second degree felony** is punishable by a sentence of imprisonment of not less than two nor more than 20 years. There are approximately 45 second degree felonies listed in the Penal Code and the Health and Safety Code. Examples include manslaughter, sexual assault, aggravated assault, and arson.

A **third degree felony** is punishable by imprisonment in a state prison for not less than two nor more than ten years. There are approximately 75 third degree felony crimes in Texas.

The fifth and lowest category of felony offense in Texas is a **state jail felony**. In most cases, a state jail felony crime is punishable by imprisonment in a state jail facility (as opposed to a state prison) for a term of not less than 180 days nor more than two years.

In addition to the terms of imprisonment that are mandated by statute for each of the above felony categories, the judge may also sentence the offender to payment of a fine of not more than $10,000. This fine is in addition to the sentence of incarceration; it is not a substitute for imprisonment.

Misdemeanor Offenses

Like felonies, misdemeanor offenses are also classified into categories by level of seriousness. There are three categories: Class A, Class B, and Class C. According to Pen §12.03(b), if an offense is listed as a misdemeanor in the statutes, but the specific class or degree of the crime is not specified, the crime is considered to be a Class C misdemeanor. The associated punishments for these crimes are defined in Pen §12.21 through Pen §12.35.

A **Class A misdemeanor** is punishable by either a term of imprisonment in a county jail for no more than one year, or by a fine of no more than $4,000, or by both the fine and term of imprisonment. Examples of Class A misdemeanors include simple assault and the burglary of a coin-operated machine. The state has steadily increased the maximum fine since 1974. Between 1974 and 1991, the maximum possible fine for this category of offense was $2,000; it was increased to $3,000 in 1991 and to $4,000 in 1994.

A **Class B misdemeanor** is by either a term of imprisonment in a county jail for no more than 180 days, or by a fine of up to $2,000, or by both the fine and jail term. Prior to 1991, the maximum fine was $1,000; it was increased to $1,500 in 1991 and to $2,000 in 1994.

A **Class C misdemeanor** is punishable by a fine of up to $500; there is no term of imprisonment associated with Class C misdemeanor offenses. There are approximately 30 different Class C offenses (not counting municipal ordinance violations and traffic tickets) listed in the Transportation Code, the Health and Safety Code, and the Penal Code.

SENTENCING HABITUAL AND/OR REPEAT OFFENDERS

According to the Texas Penal Code, offenders with prior convictions may receive more severe sentences. Pen §12.42 discusses the sentencing of repeat and habitual felony offenders; Pen §12.43 outlines sentence enhancements for repeat and habitual misdemeanor offenders. For example, if an offender convicted of a state jail felony has previously been convicted of two state jail felonies, he/she will be punished as if convicted of a third degree felony. Similarly, an offender who is convicted of a second degree felony and who has a prior felony conviction will be punished for a first degree felony.

In most cases, if the defendant is a first-time repeat offender, the punishment is increased one punishment level (e.g., from a second degree felony to a first degree felony). If the repeat offender is convicted of a first degree felony, the minimum term of imprisonment is increased to 15 years. Generally, if the defendant is a habitual offender, one who has at least two prior felony convictions, he/she is subject to a minimum term of imprisonment of 25 years and a maximum sentence of 99 years in prison or life imprisonment.

OTHER SENTENCING ALTERNATIVES

Restitution, Reparation, and Fines

Several types of sentences that may be imposed require the offender to make some type of financial payment, either to the court or to the victim. A **fine** (see Schmalleger, pp.386-388) is a monetary payment made to the state. **Restitution** (see Schmalleger, p.369) involves repaying the victim for a loss sustained as a result of the crime. **Reparation** involves compensating the victim for some harm that resulted from the crime. The death of the victim does not end the offender's requirement to pay restitution or reparation; if the victim dies before the payments are completed, all remaining payments must be made to the deceased's estate.

For some crimes, such as Class C misdemeanors, a fine may be the only penalty imposed on the offender by the court. However, as discussed above, for most crimes the court has the option of imposing both a financial penalty and a term of imprisonment upon an offender.

Texas, like most states, is attempting to increase the use of restitution and reparation. CCrP §42.037 discusses restitution, stating that:

> (a) In addition to any fine authorized by law, the court that sentences a defendant convicted of an offense may order the defendant to make restitution to any victim of the offense. If the court does not order restitution

> or orders partial restitution under this subsection, the court shall state on the record the reasons for not making the order or for the limited order.

Restitution may include returning damaged, lost, or destroyed property to a victim, paying the victim the value of the property, paying medical costs (including therapy and rehabilitation), reimbursing the victim for lost income, or paying funeral and other expenses. The actual amount of the restitution is determined by the court, which also sets a time period in which restitution must be paid. According to CCrP §42.037(g)(2), if payment is to be made in installments or within a specific period of time:

> The end of the period or the last installment may not be later than:
> (A) the end of the period of probation, if probation is ordered;
> (B) five years after the end of the term of imprisonment imposed, if the court does not order probation; or
> (C) five years after the date of sentencing in any other case.

If the court does not specify a time period, restitution must be made immediately.

Community Service

According to CCrP §42.036(a):

> A court may require a defendant, other than a defendant convicted of an offense under Sections 49.04–49.08, Penal Code, to serve all or part of a sentence of confinement or period of confinement required as a condition of community supervision in county jail by performing community service rather than by being confined in county jail unless the sentence of confinement was imposed by the jury in the case.

A sentence of **community service** (see Schmalleger, p.426) must specify the number of hours that must be served as well as the specific agency or organization for which the defendant will work. Offenders may only be sentenced to perform community service for government agencies or nonprofit organizations that meet certain specified statutory criteria. Each eight hours of community service is considered to be the equivalent of one day in jail.

Community Supervision

Community supervision or **probation** (see Schmalleger, pp.411-413) is discussed in CCrP §42.12. Community supervision is defined in CCrP §42.12 Sec 2(2) as:

> the placement of a defendant by a court under a continuum of programs and sanctions, with conditions imposed by the court for a specified period during which:
> (A) criminal proceedings are deferred without an adjudication of guilt; or
> (B) a sentence of imprisonment or confinement, imprisonment and fine, or confinement and fine, is probated and the imposition of sentence is suspended in whole or in part.

The topic of probation will be discussed in more detail in Chapter 8 of this supplement.

VICTIM'S RIGHTS AND SERVICES

General Rights of Crime Victims

According to CCrP §56.02(a), crime victims (including the guardian of a victim or the close relative of a deceased victim) are entitled to certain specified rights within the criminal justice system. These include:

(1) the right to receive from law enforcement agencies adequate protection from harm and threats of harm arising from cooperation with prosecution efforts;

(2) the right to have the magistrate take the safety of the victim or his family into consideration as an element in fixing the amount of bail for the accused;

(3) the right, if requested, to be informed of relevant court proceedings and to be informed if those court proceedings have been canceled or rescheduled prior to the event;

(4) the right to be informed, when requested, by a peace officer concerning the defendant's right to bail and the procedures in criminal investigations and by the district attorney's office concerning the general procedures in the criminal justice system, including general procedures in guilty plea negotiations and arrangements, restitution, and the appeals and parole process;

(5) the right to provide pertinent information to a probation department conducting a presentencing investigation concerning the impact of the offense on the victim and his family by testimony, written statement, or any other manner prior to any sentencing of the offender;

(6) the right to receive information regarding compensation to victims of crime...

(7) the right to be informed, upon request, of parole procedures, to participate in the parole process, to be notified, if requested, of parole proceedings concerning a defendant in the victim's case, to provide to the Board of Pardons and Paroles for inclusion in the defendant's file information to be considered by the board prior to the parole of any defendant convicted of any crime subject to this Act, and to be notified, if requested, of the defendant's release;

(8) the right to be provided with a waiting area, separate or secure from other witnesses, including the offender and relatives of the offender, before testifying in any proceeding concerning the offender; if a separate waiting area is not available, other safeguards should be taken to minimize the victim's contact with the offender and the offender's relatives and witnesses, before and during court proceedings;

(9) the right to prompt return of any property of the victim that is held by a law enforcement agency or the attorney for the state as evidence when the property is no longer required for that purpose;

(10) the right to have the attorney for the state notify the employer of the victim, if requested, of the necessity of the victim's cooperation and testimony in a proceeding that may necessitate the absence of the victim from work for good cause; and

(11) the right to counseling, on request, regarding acquired immune deficiency syndrome (AIDS) and human immunodeficiency virus (HIV) infection and testing for acquired immune deficiency syndrome (AIDS), human immunodeficiency virus (HIV) infection, antibodies to HIV, or infection with any other probable causative agent of AIDS, if the offense is an offense under Section 21.11(a)(1), 22.011, or 22.021, Penal Code.

In addition, crime victims have the right to be present at all public court proceedings that are related to the crime.

Victim Impact Statements

Schmalleger (see pp.382-386) discusses the **victim impact statement**. Victim impact statements are reports that are given to the sentencing judge and which describe the effects of the crime upon the victim. In Texas, the victim impact statement includes the following information, as mandated by CCrP §56.03(b):

- the name of the victim or victim's legal guardian, or the name of a close relative of a deceased victim
- the address and telephone number of the victim, guardian, or relative
- information on the economic loss suffered by the victim, guardian, or relative as a result of the crime
- information as to any physical or psychological injury suffered by the victim, guardian, or relative as a result of the crime
- information on any psychological services requested as a result of the crime
- information on any change in the victim's, guardian's, or relative's personal welfare or family relationships as a result of the crime
- information as to the victim's, guardian's, or relative's wishes regarding future notification of parole hearings for the defendant
- any other information that relates to the impact of the offense on the victim, guardian, or relative.

The court is not allowed to see the victim impact statement until after the defendant has been found guilty or adjudication has been deferred.

The Right to Restitution

When pronouncing sentence, the judge is required to consider imposing **victim restitution** as an element of the sentence (see Schmalleger, p.369). This generally involves requiring the offender to pay a sum of money to the victim as a consequence of the crime (e.g., reimbursement for medical expenses or lost wages). Restitution may also be in a nonmonetary form.

The defendant may be ordered to pay restitution in a lump sum or to make payments over a period of time. Restitution may be ordered even if the judge sentences the offender to a fine or a term of imprisonment in jail or prison.

Even if the judge has ordered the offender to make restitution, the victim still has the right to file a civil suit against the offender for damages that are in excess of the amount paid in restitution.

The Right to Compensation

In addition to restitution, victims may be eligible for **compensation**. The **Texas Crime Victims' Compensation Program**, which is administered by the Office of the Attorney General, provides benefits to victims and their families who have no other way to pay for expenses that result from a crime. The Crime Victims' Compensation Fund is considered to be a "last resort," to be used only if there are no other alternative sources to pay for certain specified victim expenses. Thus, if the offender is sentenced to restitution, the victim may not also receive compensation from the Fund; if the Fund compensates a victim for an expense and the offender is later ordered by the court to make restitution, the victim may be required to reimburse the fund. Similarly, if the victim receives money from a civil suit to cover crime-related expenses, he/she may have to reimburse the Fund for any prior compensation money already paid to the victim by the Fund.

To qualify for victim compensation, certain basic requirements must be met. These include:

- the crime must occur in Texas to a resident of Texas or the U.S., or must involve a Texas resident who has been victimized in a state or country that does not have compensation benefits for which the victim is eligible

- the crime must be reported to the appropriate law enforcement agency within a reasonable period of time

- the application for compensation must be filed within three years of the date of the crime

- the victim must cooperate with the police or other appropriate law enforcement agencies

Crimes covered by the Crime Victims' Compensation Fund include those involving "criminally injurious conduct." This is defined by CCRP §56.32(4) as:

> conduct that:
> (A) occurs or is attempted;
> (B) poses a substantial threat of personal injury or death;
> (C) is punishable by fine, imprisonment, or death, or would be punishable by fine, imprisonment, or death if the person engaging in the conduct possessed capacity to commit the conduct; and
> (D) does not arise out of the ownership, maintenance, or use of a motor vehicle, aircraft, or water vehicle, unless the conduct is intended to cause personal injury or death or the conduct is in violation of Section 550.021, Transportation Code, or one or more of the following sections of the Penal Code:
> (i) Section 19.04 (manslaughter);
> (ii) Section 19.05 (criminally negligent homicide);

(iii) Section 22.02 (aggravated assault);
(iv) Section 49.04 (driving while intoxicated);
(v) Section 49.05 (flying while intoxicated);
(vi) Section 49.06 (boating while intoxicated);
(vii) Section 49.07 (intoxication assault); or
(viii) Section 49.08 (intoxication manslaughter).

If the victim's behavior contributed to the crime, compensation may be reduced or denied. In addition, compensation benefits will be denied if the victim participated in the crime knowingly or willingly, if the victim is the offender or an accomplice, if the victim was incarcerated or on probation or parole for a felony that involved criminally injurious conduct at the time of the crime, or if the victim knowingly or intentionally provided the attorney general with false or forged information.

Texas provides victim compensation benefits up to a total of $50,000. Expenses which are eligible for compensation (if they are related to the crime) include medical costs, psychiatric care or counseling, loss of earnings or support, care of a child or dependent, funeral or burial expenses, crime scene clean-up, replacement costs for certain types of property, and other expenses specified by the Compensation Program.

CHAPTER 7

CAPITAL PUNISHMENT IN TEXAS

THE HISTORY OF CAPITAL PUNISHMENT IN TEXAS

Schmalleger (see p.398) briefly discusses the history of the death penalty in the United States. Between 1819 and 1923, the method of execution used in Texas was hanging and each county carried out its own executions. However, in 1923, the Texas State Legislature authorized the use of electrocution as the official method of capital punishment in the state. The Legislature also transferred the responsibility for executions to the state, with all executions to be performed at the Huntsville Unit facility. The first state-authorized electrocution was carried out on February 8, 1924 when five inmates were executed. Death Row was moved to Huntsville in 1928 and both Death Row and the state's electric chair remained there until 1965. In that year, all Death Row inmates were moved to the Ellis Unit; in 1999, inmates were moved to the Terrell Unit.

Between 1923 and 1964, a total of 361 inmates were executed by electrocution in the state. In 1972, the U.S. Supreme Court case of *Furman v. Georgia* challenged the constitutionality of capital punishment in the United States (see Schmalleger, pp.399-400). The Court ruled that the death penalty, as it was administered, constituted "cruel and unusual punishment" and therefore was a violation of the Eighth Amendment of the U.S. Constitution. The cases struck down death penalty laws throughout the country. At the time of the *Furman v. Georgia* decision, there were a total of 52 men in Texas who were under a sentence of death; all death sentences were commuted to life imprisonment by the state governor and the Texas Death Row was emptied by March, 1973.

In 1973, the Texas State Legislature revised the Penal Code, reinstating the death penalty in Texas as of January 1, 1974. The first man was placed on Death Row in February, 1974; he committed suicide later that year.

In August 1977, Texas became the first state in the U.S. to change from electrocution to lethal injection as the method of execution. The first inmate in the country to be executed by lethal injection, Charlie Brooks, was put to death in Texas on December 7, 1982.

In 1985, Texas became the first state in the country to execute a juvenile offender. Charles Rumbaugh was 17 when he committed a robbery and murder. He was executed at the age of 28.

Although close friends and relatives of the offender have historically been allowed to attend the execution, it was not until 1995 that the state gave the same right to close relatives and friends of the deceased victim. Currently, five family members or friends of the offender, as well as five family members or friends of the victim, have the right to witness the execution.

In 1998, Karla Faye Tucker became the first woman to be executed by lethal injection. She was also the first woman to be executed in Texas since 1863 and the second woman to be executed in the U.S. since the reinstatement of the death penalty in 1977.

CAPITAL PUNISHMENT IN TEXAS TODAY

Death Row in Texas

The Texas Death Row is a segregated unit located at the Terrell Unit of the Texas Department of Criminal Justice, near Livingston, Texas. Women offenders are held in a separate unit in Gatesville. The standard Death Row cell is 60 square feet and has a window, although it is not air conditioned. Inmates on Death Row do not participate in communal recreation and spend up to 23 hours per day in their cells. They are not allowed access to television but some offenders, depending on their level of custody, may be allowed a radio. There are three levels of custody, depending on the inmate's record of behavior. Inmates receive a regular diet but do not eat with the general prison population. Breakfast is at 4:00 a.m., lunch at 10:00 a.m., and dinner at 4:00 p.m.

There is limited visitation for Death Row inmates. According to CCrP §43.17, individuals allowed access to Death Row inmates include:

- his/her physician, lawyer, and clergyperson
- relatives and friends of the condemned inmate

Currently, it costs approximately $49.54 per day to incarcerate an inmate on Death Row.

Texas is one of the few states that allows inmates on Death Row to work in prison industries. Those inmates considered to be "work capable" are offered the opportunity to work in the prison's garment factory, manufacturing items such as uniforms for prison guards. Death Row inmates receive no pay for this work, although they are allowed larger, shared cells, and more visits. However, many Death Row inmates choose not to work in the prison factory.

Executions in Texas

In Texas, all executions are held after 6:00 p.m; this is mandated by CCrP §43.14. According to CCrP §43.20, attendance by witnesses is limited to the following individuals:

- the executioner (who is appointed by the Director of the Texas Department of Corrections) and any assistants
- the Board of Directors of the Texas Department of Corrections
- two physicians (including the prison physician)
- the offender's spiritual advisor
- chaplains of the Department of Corrections
- the sheriff or county judge of the county in which the Department of Corrections is located (Walker County)
- five family members or friends of the offender

In addition, five family members or friends of the deceased victim may be permitted to witness the execution. Currently, approximately half of all executions are witnessed by family or friends of the victim. The statute also states that no other convicts are allowed to witness executions.

The lethal injection used to execute inmates in Texas includes three separate drugs:

- a lethal dose of sodium thiopental which sedates the individual
- a dose of pancuronium bromide, a muscle relaxant which collapses the diaphragm and lungs
- a dose of potassium chloride which stops the heart from beating.

The total cost of the drugs used is $86.08. The entire lethal injection process lasts approximately seven minutes.

After the execution, the body of the executed inmate is embalmed and may be released upon request to a relative or friend. If no request is made within 48 hours after the execution, the body may be given to the Anatomical Board of Texas, if the Board requests the body. The Board, or the individual requesting the body, must pay a fee of $25 for embalming services. If there are no requests for the inmate's body, the inmate is buried by the state and the embalming fee is paid by the county in which the deceased inmate was originally indicted.

Death Row Statistics

As of August, 2000, there were a total of 449 offenders on Death Row. This includes 159 white males, 179 black males, 100 Hispanic males, 4 males of other races, 4 white females, and 3 black females. There were 24 juveniles on Death Row.

The average length of stay on Death Row prior to execution is 10.39 years. The longest stay on Death Row was approximately 24 years; the shortest stay was 252 days.

The average age of executed offenders is approximately 39 years. The youngest inmate to be executed was Jay Pinkerton, who was 24 years of age at the time of his execution in 1986. The oldest inmates to be executed were both 62 years old: Clydell Coleman was executed in 1999 and Betty Beets in 2000.

Since the death penalty was officially reinstated in the United States in 1976, Texas has executed more offenders than any other state in the country. Between 1977, when executions resumed throughout the United States, and the end of 1997, a total of 432 inmates were put to death in the U.S. Of these 144 (33 percent) were executed in Texas. In 1997 alone, there were 74 executions in the U.S.; 37 of these (50 percent) took place in Texas. Between 1977 and 1997, the total number of executions in Texas exceeded that in the next four states with the largest number of executions: Virginia (46 executions), Florida (39 executions), Missouri (29 executions), and Louisiana (24 executions).

Texas also has the largest Death Row Population in the U.S. Between 1976 and August 1, 2000, a total of 225 inmates have been executed in Texas. Of these, 112 were white, 75 black, 34 Hispanic, and 4 members of other races.

Capital Offenses

The only death penalty offense that has ever existed in Texas is **capital murder**. Capital murder is basically first degree murder that includes at least one of eight aggravating factors. According to Pen §19.03(a), these aggravating factors include:

(1) the person murders a peace officer or fireman who is acting in the lawful discharge of an official duty and who the person knows is a peace officer or fireman;
(2) the person intentionally commits the murder in the course of committing or attempting to commit kidnapping, burglary, robbery, aggravated sexual assault, arson, or obstruction or retaliation;
(3) the person commits the murder for remuneration or the promise of remuneration or employs another to commit the murder for remuneration or the promise of remuneration;
(4) the person commits the murder while escaping or attempting to escape from a penal institution;
(5) the person, while incarcerated in a penal institution, murders another:
  (A) who is employed in the operation of the penal institution; or
  (B) with the intent to establish, maintain, or participate in a combination or in the profits of a combination;
(6) the person:
  (A) while incarcerated for an offense under this section or Section 19.02, murders another; or
  (B) while serving a sentence of life imprisonment or a term of 99 years for an offense under Section 20.04, 22.021, or 29.03, murders another;
(7) the person murders more than one person:
  (A) during the same criminal transaction; or
  (B) during different criminal transactions but the murders are committed pursuant to the same scheme or course of conduct; or
(8) the person murders an individual under six years of age.

The minimum age to receive the death penalty in Texas is 17. Texas does not forbid the execution of mentally retarded offenders. On August 9, 2000, Oliver Cruz, a mentally retarded offender with an IQ of approximately 62, was executed in Texas.

The Death Penalty Trial and Appeal Process in Texas

In all cases involving capital murder, the accused must be indicted by a Grand Jury; a prosecutorial information is not sufficient in these cases. The accused then goes to an arraignment where he/she enters a plea. The court determines whether or not the defendant is indigent and, if so, appoints legal counsel to represent him/her. This counsel must be an attorney qualified to handle a case involving the death penalty. After pre-trial motions, a trial is held to determine the defendant's guilt or innocence of the charge of capital murder. This must be a jury trial rather than a bench trial; a defendant who is charged with a capital felony in which the state plans to seek the death penalty may not waive his/her right to a trial by jury. If the state is seeking the death penalty, the state and the defense are allowed fifteen peremptory challenges each during the jury selection phase (if the death penalty is not being sought, each side is entitled to ten such challenges).

In all capital cases, the prosecution is required to state prior to trial whether or not they plan to seek the death penalty as punishment for the crime. This information must also be provided to prospective jury members. CCrP §35.16(b)(1) states that the prosecution has the right to make a challenge for cause if:

> the juror has conscientious scruples in regard to the infliction of the punishment of death for crime, in a capital case, where the State is seeking the death penalty

If the defendant is found guilty of capital murder, the sentence will be determined. The only possible sentences in a case of capital murder are death or life imprisonment. According to CCRP §37.071(1):

> If a defendant is found guilty in a capital felony case in which the state does not seek the death penalty, the judge shall sentence the defendant to life imprisonment.

In most cases, life imprisonment means that the offender must serve at least 40 years incarceration before being eligible for parole.

If the state is seeking the death penalty, a separate sentencing hearing will be held to determine whether the defendant will be sentenced to life imprisonment or death. When possible, the sentence will be determined by the same jury that convicted him/her.

In Texas, the conviction of a capital crime, and the sentence of death, are automatically appealed to the Court of Criminal Appeals; this is mandatory and the Court does not have the discretion to refuse the appeal. The full complement of nine justices must convene for all death penalty cases. If the Court finds against the offender, a writ of certiorari may be filed to the United States Supreme Court to appeal the conviction or the sentence; this appeal must be based on United States constitutional grounds.

In Texas, the governor has the power of executive clemency, which is the right to grant a full or a conditional pardon, a full pardon based on innocence, a commutation of sentence, a remission of a fine or forfeiture that resulted from a criminal conviction, an emergency medical reprieve, or a thirty-day reprieve of execution. However, the governor can only grant executive clemency (with the exception of the thirty-day pardon) upon a recommendation from the Texas Board of Pardons and Paroles. A reprieve is not a pardon or commutation of a sentence; it merely delays or temporarily suspends punishment, including execution.

All requests for executive clemency must be filed with the Texas Board of Pardons and Paroles, which reviews the case and renders a decision on the request. If the Board recommends executive clemency, the case is passed to the state governor, who has the right to accept or reject the Board's recommendation. If the Board denies the request for clemency, a Death Row inmate has the right to request a one-time, thirty-day reprieve of execution from the state governor, who has the constitutional authority to issue such a reprieve without a recommendation from the Board. The purpose of such a reprieve is, in most cases, to give the Board additional time to conduct a full hearing on the case.

CHAPTER 8

CORRECTIONS IN TEXAS

INTRODUCTION

The agency primarily responsible for the administration of the state's correctional program, and for the supervision, punishment, rehabilitation, and reintegration of convicted offenders, is the **Texas Department of Criminal Justice** (TDCJ), which operates state prisons and state jails, administers parole, and oversees community supervision programs (formerly known as adult probation). The **Texas Board of Criminal Justice** (TBCJ) oversees the operation of the TDCJ.

PRISONS IN TEXAS

Schmalleger (pp.443-471) discusses the topic of **prisons** in detail, including the history and development of prison institutions.

The Texas Board of Criminal Justice

The **Texas Board of Criminal Justice** (TBCJ) oversees the operation of the TDCJ. The TBCJ has nine members who are appointed by the governor with the advice and consent of the state senate. One member is designated by the governor to be the chairman of the TBCJ. Members of the TBCJ serve staggered six-year terms and are not compensated for their service on the Board, although they may be reimbursed for expenses. Board members go through a training program that must comply with the requirements outlined in Section 492.0031 of the Government Code (GC). These include providing the member with information on:

- the legislation that created the TDCJ and the TBCJ
- programs operated by the TDCJ
- the roles and functions of the TDCJ
- the rules of the TDCJ
- the TDCJ current budget
- the results of the most recent formal audit of the TDCJ
- the requirements of various laws relating to public officials
- all applicable ethics policies

The Board has a variety of responsibilities, including hiring the executive director of the TDCJ and setting department rules and policies. The Board also acts as the Board of Trustees for the Windham School System, which is located within the TDCJ; they hire the school system superintendent and provide general guidance and oversight. The Board, which is headquartered in Austin, meets at least four times a year.

The Texas Department of Criminal Justice

The **Texas Department of Criminal Justice** (TDCJ) is the state agency responsible for the oversight of all inmates held in state correctional facilities. In most cases, the Department is responsible only for adult offenders: individuals who are at least 17 years of age. The Department operates state prisons, state jails, and state parole, as well as overseeing community supervision.

The mission of the Department is stated in GC §493.001:

> The mission of the department is to provide public safety, promote positive change in offender behavior, reintegrate offenders into society, and assist victims of crime.

The Department is divided into a number of divisions:

1. institutional division
2. community justice assistance division
3. parole division
4. state jail division
5. internal audit division
6. programs and services division
7. financial services division
8. general counsel TDCJ
9. public information division
10. victim services division
11. health services division

The Institutional Division

The **Institutional Division** is the largest division in the Department and is responsible for the operation and management of the state prison system. As of August 31, 1998, the division operated a total of 58 state prison facilities, including 52 prison units, three psychiatric facilities, two medical facilities and a mentally retarded offender program. In addition, there are two additional medical facilities, two boot camps, and three work camps located within these facilities. The division also has contracts to house offenders in seven private prisons.

The division was responsible for over 132,273 offenders as of August 31, 1998. Of these offenders, 94 percent were male and 6 percent female. Approximately 45 percent of the incarcerated offenders were black, 29 percent white, and 26 percent Hispanic. The average age was 34.6 years

The standard prison unit routine begins with a wake-up call at 3:30 a.m. Inmates eat breakfast at 4:30 a.m. and report to work assignments at 6:00 a.m. All physically-capable inmates have job assignments; most work in prison support jobs such as cooking, cleaning, laundry, and maintenance. They do not receive pay for this work but earn privileges for good work habits and learn job skills which may help them find a job after they are released from prison. Approximately 10,000 inmates are employed in the prison system's agricultural program, which produces food, livestock, and cotton on prison farms and ranches. In addition, approximately 8,000 offenders are employed in the state's prison industries program.

The division provides a variety of educational opportunities for incarcerated offenders. All offenders with less than a seventh grade education are required by law to attend school in prison and to work towards a GED. Offenders with at least a seventh grade education, but who do not have a high school diploma, are encouraged to finish their GED; however, for these offenders, school is a privilege that must be earned through good behavior and satisfactory performance in their prison work assignment. In addition to GED programs, the division also provides a variety of vocational classes. These classes are offered through the Windham School District, which is the only fully accredited school system within a prison in the United States. Approximately 60,000 offenders are enrolled in academic courses and 16,000 in vocational courses. The school awards approximately 9,000 GEDs and 8,000 vocational certificates each year. In addition, those offenders who have completed high school or earned a GED may be given the opportunity to take college courses, which are offered through a contract arrangement between the state and various junior colleges throughout Texas. Offenders who earn the privilege of taking college courses must, upon release on parole or mandatory supervision, reimburse the state for the tuition of these courses.

Offenders incarcerated in state prison units receive all essential items from the prison. Inmates may open a trust account into which family and friends may deposit money; these funds may be used by the inmates to make purchases of snack foods, toiletries, magazines, and books from the unit commissary. Profits from the commissaries are used to purchase color televisions to place in unit dayrooms. In most units, offenders do not have televisions in their cells.

While all prison units in Texas have heating units, only the hospital and psychiatric units have air conditioning during the summer months. Other units have forced air systems to keep inside air moving and bring in fresh air. Ironically, those offenders who are housed in single cell administrative segregation units (to isolate them from the general prison population because of gang membership, violent behavior, etc.) also have air conditioning. This is because the windows in these cells cannot be opened due to a security concern that weapons or other contraband could be smuggled into these restricted areas through the open window. Thus, in a direct contradiction to the divisional philosophy that privileges must be earned, those offenders housed in administrative segregation for poor behavior have the privilege of air conditioning while offenders housed in the general population do not have this privilege.

The Community Justice Assistance Division

The **Community Justice Assistance Division** is responsible for administering community supervision in Texas. In 1989, the Legislature officially changed the term "adult probation" to "community supervision." This division works with community supervision and corrections departments that oversee those offenders who are serving their sentence in the community, rather than serving a sentence of incarceration. Probation/community supervision in Texas is discussed in more detail later in this chapter.

The Parole Division

The **Parole Division** of the TDCJ is responsible for supervising those offenders who have been released from prison and who are serving the remainder of their sentence in the community. The division is also responsible for certain pre-release programs, such as the pre-parole transfer program and the work program. The division is not responsible for making release or revocation decisions or for assigning special conditions of parole. Parole in Texas is discussed in more detail later in this chapter.

The State Jail Division

The **State Jail Division** of the TDCJ was created in 1993 to provide a way to incarcerate certain low-level felony offenders. The length of time that may be served in a state jail ranges from 180 days to two years. There are no good time provisions for early release, and offenders may not be granted parole from a state jail facility. State jails also serve as transfer facilities for minimum security offenders awaiting transfer from a local county jail to a state prison unit.

There are a total of 17 state jail facilities throughout the state; twelve are state operated while five are private contract facilities that are supervised by the state jail division. These facilities have a total capacity of 25,490 beds. In 1998, approximately 10,000 state jail felons and 13,000 transfer-status offenders were housed in state jails. Upon admission to a state jail facility, each offender is individually evaluated and an individual treatment plan is designed to facilitate offender rehabilitation. While in these facilities, offenders may receive substance abuse awareness and prevention education, academic and vocational training, and life skills education. Offenders also participate in community service work programs.

The Victim Services Division

The **Victim Services Division** provides services to victims and their families to ensure them the opportunity to participate in all phases of the criminal justice system. CCrP §56.02 is known as the Bill of Rights for Texas Crime Victims and outlines the rights of victims, their guardians, and close relatives of deceased victims. Sections of this statute are quoted in Chapter 6 of this Supplement.

The division provides a variety of services to victims. The **Victim Notification System** provides written notification to victims of an offender's status after conviction and sentencing. In fiscal year 1998, the division mailed out over 30,000 letters to victims and concerned citizens listed on the notification database. The division also operates an **Automated Victim Notification Service** which allows victims and their families to obtain offender status information over the telephone at any time. The division has implemented **Victim Impact Panels** to assist victims with recovery. These panels are composed of crime victims who are willing to share their victimization experiences with others. Participation on such panels often assists victims in their own recovery, as well as providing audience members with increased awareness and victim sensitivity. **Prison tours** are conducted for victims, their families, and members of the criminal justice system, to provide education in the conditions of incarceration in Texas. The **Texas Crime Victim Clearinghouse** coordinates victim services and serves as a central information source about victim services and issues throughout the state. It produces a Victim Assistance Resource Directory and maintains statistics on victim impact statements. The Victim Offender Mediation/Dialogue program is designed for victims of violent crime who request the opportunity to meet the offender. Offenders must have admitted their guilt prior to the meeting, and the mediation is not included in the parole file (to ensure that offenders are not participating merely as a way to increase their chances of receiving parole). The program provides victims with the opportunity to talk with the offender and ask questions, as well as giving offenders the opportunity to become responsible and accountable for their own behavior.

Other Divisions
The **Internal Audit Division** is responsible for assisting in the annual audit of the TDCJ. The results are reported directly to the TBCJ. In addition, the division reviews draft agency policies, serves on various agency committees, and provides various other types of assistance to management. The **Programs and Services Division**, which was created in 1995, coordinates activities among the various divisions of the Department. The division focuses on programs such as the Windham School District, the Substance Abuse Treatment Program, and the Sex Offender Treatment Program, which are implemented across divisions, to ensure that these programs are administered efficiently and consistently. The **Financial Services Division** is responsible for the fiscal management of the TDJC.

The **Office of the General Counsel** is the legal arm of the TDCJ and provides legal support and services to the Department. Duties include providing legal consultation to the Board, coordinating litigation activity, assisting in the preparation of Department policy, and assisting in any other legal matters. The Office also acts as a liaison between the Department and the Office of the State Attorney General, and between the Department and the courts. The **Health Services Division** is responsible for ensuring that incarcerated offenders receive quality health care. The division monitors all health care delivery throughout the TDCJ.

PRISON LABOR

Schmalleger discusses the issue of prison labor and prison industries on pp.450-452. The prison industries program in the TDCJ is known as **Texas Correctional Industries** (TCI). TCI provides a variety of products and services to the Department, to state government agencies, and to agencies of local governments. The agency also provides offenders with opportunities for rehabilitation and job training skills.

TCI, which was originally the Industrial Division of the TDCJ, was created in 1963 and given the right to sell prison-made goods to tax-supported agencies and political subdivisions within the state of Texas. According to GC §497.002(a), the purposes of TCI include:

> (1) provide work program participants with marketable job skills to help reduce recidivism through a coordinated program of:
> (A) job skills training;
> (B) documentation of work history; and
> (C) access to resources provided by Project RIO and the Texas Workforce Commission, including access to resources provided through assistance to local workforce development boards in referring work program participants to the Project RIO employment referral services provided under Section 306.002, Labor Code; and
> (2) reduce department costs by providing products and articles for the department and providing products or articles for sale on a for-profit basis to the public or to agencies of the state or political subdivisions of the state.

TCI has 46 factories in correctional facilities throughout Texas. Approximately 8,000 offenders are employed in these factories, producing over $100 million worth of products and services. Products produced in these factories include offender and correctional officer clothing, shoes, mattresses, license plates, furniture, textiles, janitorial and laundry supplies, park equipment, food service equipment, furniture, and traffic control signs. Services include furniture refinishing, school bus renovation, dump truck repair, tire repairs and retreading, and microfilming for state agencies. Products and services produced by TCI may be purchased by state agencies, political subdivisions, TDCJ employees, members of the Texas state legislature, other states, the federal government, foreign governments, and agencies of these governments. Private individuals may not purchase TCI products and services. TCI products and services may not be sold on the open market

In addition to TCI, incarcerated offenders may be employed in a variety of other tasks. Inmates provide much of the prison support, working at jobs such as maintenance, laundry, cooking, and cleaning within the prison units. The prison system's agricultural program, which has 139,000 acres of farm and ranch land, produces edible crops, livestock, and cotton worth approximately $50 million. In addition, prison units that do not have enough arable land to participate in this program still run small farms or gardens and produce fresh vegetables which are donated to local food banks. In fiscal year 1998, prison units donated almost 3 million pounds of vegetables for distribution to low-income families throughout Texas.

Low-risk offenders may be assigned to work outside prison units, supervised by armed correctional officers. Because of their low-risk status, these offenders are not placed on chain gangs. In 1998, offenders in prisons and state jail facilities contributed over three million hours to public service projects throughout the state. Based on a standard minimum wage, this work saved the state over $15.5 million. Service projects included cleaning storm damage from rivers and creeks, removing asbestos from public school buildings, and building homes for Habitat of Humanity. Offenders also set up playgrounds, clear state land, clean beaches and state parks, and work on baseball fields.

JAILS IN TEXAS

Jails in Texas may be operated either by a county or by a municipality, or by a private agency under a vendor contract (see Schmalleger, pp.472-480). Jails have four primary functions:

- to book arrested suspects
- to house some defendants awaiting trial (those who were not granted pretrial release)
- to incarcerate convicted offenders who are sentenced to incarceration in a local facility
- to hold inmates awaiting transfer to other facilities

Jails in Texas are regulated by the **Texas Commission on Jail Standards**. The commission, which was created in 1975, establishes minimum standards for the construction, maintenance, and operation of jails (including the custody, care and treatment of inmates), ensures that jails comply with these state-wide standards, and provides training and technical assistance in the areas of jail construction and management.

As of July 1, 2000, the total jail population in Texas was 62,479. The total jail capacity in the state was 72,912; thus, overall, jails in Texas averaged 86 percent of capacity. Approximately one dozen jails had at least 100 available beds.

COMMUNITY SUPERVISION PROGRAMS IN TEXAS

Schmalleger discusses the concept of community-based corrections programs in Chapter 11. In Texas, offenders placed on some form of community-based supervision are supervised by the TDCJ. Those offenders on parole are supervised by the Parole Division, whereas offenders on community supervision (probation) are supervised by the Community Justice Assistance Division

Parole

Schmalleger discuses the general concept of **parole** on pp.414-417. On p.414, he defines parole as "the supervised early release of inmates from correctional confinement." Parole itself is not a sentence; it is a form of early release from a sentence of incarceration. The offender serves a portion of his/her sentence under supervision in the community. He/she must report to a parole officer on a regular schedule and must obey specified conditions of release until the sentence is completed.

There are two main types of released offenders who are supervised by the TDCJ's **Parole Division**. The first category is **mandatory supervision**; this is a type of release from prison that is provided for certain categories of offenders. Offenders eligible for mandatory supervision will be released when the amount of time served and their good time credit combined equals the length of their prison sentence (their "minimum expiration date"). Until 1996, mandatory supervision release was automatic; all offenders who are incarcerated for offenses committed prior to August 31, 1996, and who are eligible for mandatory supervision, must be released on their minimum expiration date. However, in 1995, the Legislature gave the **Texas Board of Pardons and Paroles** (BPP) the right to review and intervene in mandatory supervision releases of offenders who are incarcerated for offenses committed on or after September 1, 1996. The BPP has the right to deny mandatory supervision release if it decides that the offender's release would endanger the public.

Parolees are released upon approval of the BPP; parole release is discretionary and always involves a decision by the Board. An offender's initial parole eligibility date may occur well before his/her mandatory supervision date; however, the BPP is not required to approve parole at any parole review hearing.

Regardless of which type of release the offender receives, he/she must report to a parole officer on a regular schedule, must obey specified rules and conditions of release (and be subject to arrest and re-incarceration for violation of these conditions), and must remain in the custody of the state until sentence is completed. Both categories of releasees are supervised by the Parole Division.

As of January, 1999, 76,669 releasees were being supervised by Texas parole officers.

The Texas Board of Pardons and Paroles

The **Texas Board of Pardons and Paroles** (BPP) is the agency responsible for determining whether eligible inmates are released into the community under some type of parole supervision. The BPP also determines the conditions of release and responds to any violations of those conditions. In addition, the BPP makes recommendations to the governor on executive clemency matters (pardons, reprieves, and commutations).

The BPP is composed of 18 members who are appointed by the governor, with the advice and consent of the Senate, and who serve six-year terms. To be eligible to serve on the Board, a prospective member must be representative of the general public, be a resident citizen of Texas, and have been resident in the state for at least two years prior to appointment.

The Parole Division

The Parole Division of the TDCJ is responsible for supervising releasees who are completing their sentences in the community. The Division has a number of pre-release functions as well, including investigation of parole plans proposed by incarcerated offenders and tracking cases eligible for parole and submitting them to the Board of Pardons and Paroles. The Division also supervises inmates who are participating in two pre-release programs. The **Pre-Parole Transfer Program** provides inmates who are within one year of their parole or mandatory supervision release date with counseling, substance abuse education, and life skills and vocational training. Participants are transferred to a community-based pre-parole facility while in this program. The **Work Program** allows certain inmates to live in a secure facility while employed by private industries. Inmates must be between six months and two years of parole eligibility to participate in the work program. They receive either minimum wage or the prevailing wage for similar work in the location of the facility and must contribute up to 80 percent of their wages to cover the costs of supervision and housing, pay victim restitution and dependant support, and maintain a savings account.

The Division is not responsible for deciding who is released, for assigning release conditions, or for revoking parole; these decisions are the responsibility of the Board of Pardons and Paroles. However, the Division does assist the board by providing them with information necessary to make these determinations.

The Process of Release and Supervision

Several months before an offender reaches his/her parole eligibility review date, he/she will be interviewed by a parole officer, who prepares a case summary. This document includes the facts of the case, the offender's disciplinary record in prison, his/her physical and mental conditions, any other relevant information (e.g., assaultive behavior), and a summary of positive and negative factors. The offender provides the parole officer with his/her release plan, which includes where he/she will live upon release, any prospective employment, and any other plans (e.g., drug/alcohol treatment).

The offender's case is then reviewed by a BPP parole panel. One or more members of the panel may interview the offender prior to the panel; however, this is at the discretion of the individual members. In most cases, the panel consists of three BBP members; a majority vote is required for parole to be granted. Certain categories of offenders may only be granted parole upon a two-thirds majority vote of the entire BPP. The BPP is never required to grant release.

The Parole Division is required to notify the following officials prior to an offender's parole review or scheduled release date:

- the trial officials of the county of conviction (sentencing judge, sheriff, district attorney)
- the police chiefs of every city in the county of conviction
- the county in which the offense was convicted (in cases which included a change of venue)
- the county to which the offender will be released
- any victims or other persons who completed a victim impact statement at the time of trial or who requested notification

All offenders released on parole or mandatory supervision are required to obey certain rules of release and may have their release revoked for violation of these rules. Rules of release include (but are not limited to):

- report regularly to an assigned parole officer
- obey all local, county, state, and federal laws
- obtain written permission from the parole officer before changing residence or leaving the state
- do not own, possess, sell, or control any firearm or other prohibited or illegal weapon, do not unlawfully carry any weapon, and do not use, attempt to use, or threaten to use any object to injure or attempt to injure another person
- do not associate with persons of criminal background or with any person or group prohibited by written instruction of the parole officer
- do not enter into agreements to act as informer or special agent for any law enforcement agent without specific written approval of the Parole Division
- abide by any special conditions of release imposed by the DPP

Special release conditions that may be imposed by the BPP may include (but are not limited to):

- halfway house placement
- intensive supervision
- electronic monitoring
- drug monitoring
- mandatory participation in drug/alcohol treatment programs, psychological counseling, or educational programs

The BPP may also require violent offenders to participate in a **Super-Intensive Supervision Program** (SISP) as a special condition of release. This program provides a higher level of supervision for potentially dangerous offenders as a way of protecting the public safety. All offenders released into SISP are supervised through some type of electronic monitoring and must comply with 24-hour schedules that are pre-approved by a parole officer in writing. Offenders meeting one or more of the following criteria are considered for SISP placement:

- a current or past conviction for a violent offense
- a current or past conviction for an attempted violent offense
- a current or past conviction (including juvenile convictions) for any offense that involved the threat of violence that could result in bodily injury

Electronic Monitoring of Parolees

Electronic monitoring allows additional supervision of releasees (see Schmalleger, pp.427-428). It is used primarily for those releasees requiring a higher level of supervision. Texas began using electronic monitoring in 1987. Currently there three types of electronic monitoring systems in use in the state. **Continuous electronic monitoring** requires the offender to wear a radio transmitter around his/her ankle and to have a receiving unit attached to a telephone line in his/her home. If the releasee moves more than a specified distance from the receiving unit, a central monitoring station notifies a parole officer of the violation. **Drive-by electronic monitoring** also requires the offender to wear the ankle transmitter. However, the releasee is monitored by the parole officer using a portable receiver; this allows surveillance when the releasee is not actually at home. Finally, **video monitoring** requires the releasee to telephone the central monitoring station from a designated telephone at scheduled and random times during the day. A computer uses a sample of the releasee's voice to determine if the caller matches the sample. Violations occur if the voice of the caller does not match the sample, if the releasee fails to call in at his/her scheduled time, or if he/she does not call from the designated location.

Community Supervision (Probation)

Schmalleger (see pp.411-413, pp.415-417, and pp.421-422) discusses the general issue of **probation**. He defines probation on p.411 as "a sentence served while under supervision in the community." In Texas, adult probation is known as **community supervision**, by an order of the Texas Legislature in 1989. Community supervision is different from parole in that offenders sentenced to community supervision serve their sentences in the community whereas parolees are offenders who have already served some portion of their sentence in prison. According to CCRP §42.12, Sec. 2(2):

> "Community supervision" means the placement of a defendant by a court under a continuum of programs and sanctions, with conditions imposed by the court for a specified period during which:
> (A) criminal proceedings are deferred without an adjudication of guilt; or
> (B) a sentence of imprisonment or confinement, imprisonment and fine, or confinement and fine, is probated and the imposition of sentence is suspended in whole or in part.

Parole, on the other hand, involves the conditional release of an offender from the custody of the TDCJ's Institutional Division, to serve the remainder of his/her sentence under the control and supervision of the Parole Division.

Community supervision services are administered by the **Community Justice Assistance Division** of the TDCJ, which works with community supervision and corrections departments that supervise offenders. Currently, over 440,000 offenders are on community supervision in Texas; this includes approximately 251,000 felons and 189,000 misdemeanor offenders.

Community Supervision and Corrections Departments (CSCDs) are responsible for the direct supervision and rehabilitation of offenders sentenced to community supervision. Currently, there are 122 CSCDs in Texas, serving all 254 counties. CSCDs receive funding from the Community Justice Assistance Division of the TDJC but are not part of the division. They are organized within the state's local judicial districts and receive support from the district. CSCD employees work for the judicial district whereas Division employees work for the state of Texas. The Community Justice Assistance Division is responsible for monitoring CSCDs but does not work directly with offenders. Instead, it tracks CSCD performance, reviews budgets, distributes state funding, enforces mandatory standards of community supervision, and provides training and certification of community supervision officers.

After being sentenced to community supervision, each offender is assigned a community supervision officer. This officer designs an individualized supervision program for the offender, which includes any conditions the court required at sentencing (see Schmalleger, p.412-413). CSCD officers have a variety of tools available to supervise and rehabilitate offenders and to protect the public. These include, but are not limited to:

- physical equipment (e.g., electronic monitoring, urinalysis testing)
- special facilities (e.g., local boot camps, restitution centers, day reporting centers, residential treatment centers)
- multiple levels of supervision (e.g., basic supervision, intensive supervision)
- specialized caseloads targeting sex offenders, substance abusers, or offenders with special needs (e.g., mentally or physically disabled offenders)
- rehabilitation programs (e.g., continuing education, vocational training, cognitive skills training, life skills training, substance abuse treatment)
- victim notification program to provide information and support to victims of offenders on community supervision.

In some cases, the court may require an offender to live in a residential facility while on community supervision. This provides a higher level of supervision but does not use up scarce prison space on non-violent offenders. There are several types of residential facilities for offenders on community supervision. **Boot camps**, which resemble a military basic training program, focus on young, first-time offenders. In addition to strict supervision, discipline, and physical exercise, they provide general education, life skills training, and substance abuse education, and require offenders to make restitution both to their victims and to society.

Offenders who have been ordered to pay restitution may be required to live in a **restitution center** if they have difficulty keeping a job or paying restitution, or if they have substance abuse problems. Offenders living in these centers must get and keep a full-time job, perform community service restitution (essentially volunteer work in the community), and attend education and life skills training classes.

Offenders with drug or alcohol problems may be assigned to a **court residential treatment center** to receive treatment. These centers also provide education and life skills training and may also offer vocational and employment assistance. **Substance abuse treatment facilities** also provide treatment and rehabilitation of offenders with drug or alcohol problems. Finally, offenders who violate court-ordered conditions of community supervision may be sent to an **intermediate sanctions facility** rather than having his/her supervision revoked and sending him/her to prison.

BECOMING A CORRECTIONAL OFFICER

Schmalleger discusses the concept of the professionalization of correctional officers on pp.501-503 and discusses the job of probation and parole officers on pp.422-423. To become a correctional officer in Texas, applicants must meet certain minimum eligibility criteria. These include:

- U.S. citizen or alien authorized to work in the U.S.
- minimum age of 18
- high school diploma from a state-accredited school or state-issued GED
- not be on active military duty
- no felony convictions
- no convictions for drug-related offense (an alcohol-related offense is not considered a drug-related offense)
- no convictions for any offense involving domestic violence
- no Class A or B misdemeanor convictions in the last 5 years
- not on probation for any criminal offense
- no criminal charges pending
- no outstanding warrants
- if male and between the ages of 18 and 25, must be registered with Selective Service if required by law
- be able to perform all essential functions of a correctional officer, with or without reasonable accommodation

Applicants must pass a TDCJ pre-employment test, a TDCJ drug test, and a background screening. If selected by the TDCJ, applicants go through a training program at the TDCJ Correctional Officer Training Academy in Beeville (near Corpus Christi) or at one of the other academies located around the state. Trainees attending the Beeville and Gatesville academies receive free room and board. Training includes approximately 160 hours of instruction over 40 weeks. It includes training in firearms, self defense, chemical agents, first aid and CPR, physical training, non-violent crisis intervention, and standards for use of force.

The basic eligibility criteria for parole caseworkers are similar but not identical. They include:

- U.S. citizen or alien authorized to work in the U.S.
- minimum age of 18

- bachelor's degree (from an institution of higher education accredited by the Council for Higher Education) in criminal justice, criminology, corrections, counseling, law, social work, psychology, sociology, or a related field approved by the Parole Division, or
- if the degree is not in one of the listed disciplines, the applicant must have either one year of graduate study in one of the listed disciplines or one year experience in full-time casework, counseling, or community or group work approved by the Parole Division
- no convictions for family violence
- not be on active military duty
- not be on probation for any criminal offense
- no criminal charges pending
- no outstanding warrants
- at least 15 years since the completion of any sentence (including probation) for a felony conviction
- if male and between the ages of 18 and 25, must be registered with Selective Service if required by law
- be able to perform all essential functions of a parole caseworker, with or without reasonable accommodation

Applicants must submit to mandatory drug testing and a background check. Caseworkers spend one month in an on-the-job training program prior to attending the Parole Caseworker Training Academy in Austin for two weeks. Academy training includes instruction on administrative responsibilities and the policies and procedures of the Parole Division.

CHAPTER 9

THE JUVENILE JUSTICE SYSTEM IN TEXAS

INTRODUCTION

Schmalleger discusses the concept of juvenile justice and juvenile crime in Chapter 14. The definition of a **juvenile** in Texas is similar to that of many other states. Family Code (FC) §51.02(2) states that a:

> "Child" means a person who is:
> (A) ten years of age or older and under 17 years of age; or
> (B) seventeen years of age or older and under 18 years of age who is alleged or found to have engaged in delinquent conduct or conduct indicating a need for supervision as a result of acts committed before becoming 17 years of age.

FC §51.03.(a) defines **delinquent conduct** as

> (1) conduct, other than a traffic offense, that violates a penal law of this state or of the United States punishable by imprisonment or by confinement in jail;
> (2) conduct that violates a reasonable and lawful order of a juvenile court entered under Section 54.04 or 54.05 of this code, except an order prohibiting the following conduct:
> (A) a violation of the penal laws of this state of the grade of misdemeanor that is punishable by fine only or a violation of the penal ordinances of any political subdivision of this state;
> (B) the unexcused voluntary absence of a child from school; or
> (C) the voluntary absence of a child from his home without the consent of his parent or guardian for a substantial length of time or without intent to return;
> (3) conduct that violates a lawful order of a municipal court or justice court under circumstances that would constitute contempt of that court;
> (4) conduct that violates Section 49.04, 49.05, 49.06, 49.07, or 49.08, Penal Code; or
> (5) conduct that violates Section 106.041, Alcoholic Beverage Code, relating to driving under the influence of alcohol by a minor (third or subsequent offense).

Essentially, under this law, juvenile delinquency involves either a violation of the Texas Penal Code or a violation of court-ordered conditions of juvenile probation.

Texas also recognizes the concept of **status offender**, which is defined in FC §51.02(15) as:

> a child who is accused, adjudicated, or convicted for conduct that would not, under state law, be a crime if committed by an adult, including:
> (A) truancy under Section 51.03(b)(2);

(B) running away from home under Section 51.03(b)(3);
(C) a fineable only offense under Section 51.03(b)(1) transferred to the juvenile court under Section 51.08(b), but only if the conduct constituting the offense would not have been criminal if engaged in by an adult;
(D) failure to attend school under Section 25.094, Education Code;
(E) a violation of standards of student conduct as described by Section 51.03(b)(5);
(F) a violation of a juvenile curfew ordinance or order;
(G) a violation of a provision of the Alcoholic Beverage Code applicable to minors only; or
(H) a violation of any other fineable only offense under Section 8.07(a)(4) or (5), Penal Code, but only if the conduct constituting the offense would not have been criminal if engaged in by an adult.

In 1999, a total of 154,650 juveniles between the ages of ten and 17 were arrested by police in Texas. Of these, 61,026 were warned and released, handled in justice and municipal courts, or diverted out of the juvenile justice system; 93,624 were referred to juvenile probation departments. In addition, 25,372 juveniles were referred by other sources, such as social agencies, parents, schools, and the Texas Youth Commission. The total number of referrals (118,996) is a decrease of 5.3 percent from 1998.

Approximately 55 percent of the juveniles referred to juvenile probation departments had been referred before. About 23 percent had been previously adjudicated by the courts and almost 1 percent had previously been committed to the Texas Youth Commission. Between 1996 and 1999, the percent of total referrals with no prior referral has increased, while repeat referrals has declined.

THE HISTORY OF JUVENILE JUSTICE IN TEXAS

Schmalleger (pp.538-545) discusses the history of the juvenile justice system in the United States. The state of Texas has treated juveniles different from adult offenders since the mid-1850s, when the state legislature passed a law exempting juveniles who were under the age of 13 from criminal prosecution in certain situations. The legislature also authorized the construction of a separate correctional facility to house juveniles. Although construction was delayed by the outbreak of the Civil War, the **Gatesville State School for Boys** was opened in 1889, and the **Gainesville State School** (for girls) opened in 1916. Until 1920, all state facilities for juveniles were independently run and reported to the state governor. Between 1920 and 1949, these facilities were run by the **Texas Board of Control.**

In 1949, the state legislature created the **Texas Youth Development Council**, which coordinated efforts to develop community-based youth services and administered juvenile training schools in Texas. In 1957, administration of all state juvenile training schools and all homes for neglected and dependent children was handed over to the **Texas Youth Council**. In 1961, this agency also began providing parole services for delinquent youth. During the 1960s and the 1970s, juvenile justice services in Texas focused attention on the development of community-based alternatives to institutional delivery of services. A county juvenile probation subsidy program was created, which was eventually made the responsibility of the **Texas Juvenile Probation Commission**, created in

1981. Several landmark Texas and U.S. Supreme Court cases eventually led the Texas Legislature to enact Title 3 of the Texas Family Code in 1973. This section is now known as the **Juvenile Justice Code**.

In 1983, the Texas Youth Council was renamed the **Texas Youth Commission** (TYC). In the mid-1980s, Texas experienced a sharp increase in the rate of juvenile crime in the state. Between 1988 and 1993, referrals to juvenile probation for delinquent activity increased 61 percent while referrals for violent offenses increased 161 percent. The rate of homicides in Texas rose to 12.8 per 100,000, almost twice the national rate of 6.6 per 100,000. In addition, there was a 285 percent increase in the number of juveniles committed to the TYC for violent crimes.

In 1987, in response to this increase in violent juvenile crime, Texas adopted **blended sentencing**. This technique combines a criminal sentence and a traditional juvenile court disposition, allowing juveniles who are given determinate sentences to serve the first part of the sentence in TYC and later be transferred to the adult system to complete the sentence.

Between 1990 and 1998, the proportion of total arrested suspects in Texas who were juveniles increased from 23 percent to 35 percent. In addition, arrests for juvenile violent crime increased. TYC commitments increased along with the increased rate of juvenile crime. In fiscal year 1993, there were 1,564 new commitments; this number increased 104 percent by fiscal year 1998, when there were 3,188 new commitments to TYC.

In 1995, the Texas Legislature passed juvenile reform legislation emphasizing the "get tough, balanced approach" which combined punishment with rehabilitation for juvenile offenders. Elements of this legislation, which became effective in January, 1996, included:

- adding the concept of "punishment" as a purpose of the Juvenile Justice Code

- reducing the certification age to 14 (from 15) for capital felonies and first degree felonies; once a juvenile is certified, he/she will automatically be transferred to adult criminal court for all subsequent felony offenses

- expansion of determinate sentencing - eleven new offenses (all violent crimes against persons) were added to the original five

- increasing the range of possible sentences to a maximum of 40 years for first degree felonies and establishing minimum confinement periods for sentenced juvenile offenders

- authorizing TYC to request the juvenile court transfer sentenced juveniles after age 16 to adult prison for completion of sentence

- requiring all sentenced youth to complete sentences after age 21 (in some cases age 19) on adult parole

- requiring all referrals to juvenile court for felonies and misdemeanors involving violence or weapons to be reviewed by the prosecuting attorney for possible prosecution

In the late 1990s, juvenile crime rates began to level off and commitments to TYC showed a slight decline, with a drop of 7 percent between fiscal year 1998 and fiscal year 1999.

THE TEXAS JUVENILE JUSTICE SYSTEM TODAY

The **Texas Juvenile Justice System** includes elements at both the state and local levels, each with specific functions and responsibilities.

State Agencies

There are two main agencies at the state level which deal with juvenile justice. The **Texas Juvenile Probation Commission** (TJPC) was created in 1981 and is responsible for coordinating all juvenile probation services throughout the state, setting and maintaining minimum state standards, and ensuring that effective probation services are available to juveniles throughout Texas. The **Texas Youth Commission** (TYC) , which was originally created in 1949 as the Texas Youth Development Council, is responsible for juvenile correctional institutions throughout Texas, providing care, custody and rehabilitation for violent and chronic juvenile offenders who are committed to secure custody.

There are several other state agencies which are involved in the juvenile justice system. The **Texas Department of Mental Health and Mental Retardation** provides services to juveniles who are mentally ill or mentally retarded and who either are found to be not competent to stand trial or found not responsible for their conduct. The **Texas Department of Protective and Regulatory Services** is responsible for providing a variety of services to neglected and abused children, and to at-risk children and their families. The **Texas Department of Public Safety** operates the Juvenile Justice Information System, a state-wide computer database collecting information regarding the arrest, adjudication, and disposition of juvenile offenders.

Local Agencies

There are a large number of local-level agencies which are involved in the juvenile justice system. Each county in Texas has a **County Juvenile Board** which oversees the juvenile justice system at the local level. Members of the board generally include all district court judges, county court judges, and statutory court judges. The board hires the Chief Juvenile Probation Officer for the county and is responsible for making budget and policy decisions for the county's juvenile probation department. There are 172 boards in Texas (some boards cover multiple counties). **Juvenile court judges** are also selected by board. Currently, there are 407 juvenile court judges in Texas. The **County Juvenile Probation Department** deals with approximately 97 percent of all juveniles who commit crimes; only about 3 percent are committed to the TYC. There are over 160 juvenile probation departments in Texas.

The **County Commissioner's Court** provides funding to the juvenile justice system. Each county also has a **Juvenile Prosecutor** or **Juvenile Prosecuting Attorney**, who is usually an Assistant District Attorney or Assistant County Attorney (depending on local preference). **Justice** and **Municipal Court Judges** are heavily involved in the juvenile justice system because they handle most Class C misdemeanors and ordinance violations committed by juveniles, as well as cases such as truancy and failure to attend school. When juvenile court judges are unavailable, justice and municipal court judges will frequently magistrate juvenile offenders (the procedural equivalent of Miranda warnings) and conduct detention hearings. **Local law enforcement officers** investigate criminal offenses by juveniles and arrest juvenile offenders. Finally, **volunteers** are used in many counties in areas such as mediation, victim-offender programs, mentoring, restitution, and prevention programs.

WHAT HAPPENS TO A JUVENILE WHO BREAKS THE LAW IN TEXAS?

A juvenile who breaks the law in Texas enters the Texas **juvenile justice system**. This system differs in several key ways from the adult criminal justice system (see Schmalleger, pp.562-563). Schmalleger (see p.562) provides a diagram of the general juvenile justice process. This is similar to the process used in Texas.

Many of the juveniles caught breaking the law are charged with minor crimes or status offenses. Approximately one-third are serious offenders who have committed crimes such as murder, assault, or burglary. About 50 percent of all arrested juveniles are between 14 and 15 years of age and approximately 75 percent are male.

If the police catch a juvenile engaged in a minor violation of the law, the officer may choose to simply warn the child and his/her parents. If the crime is more serious, or if additional action is required to protect either the child or the public, or to prevent future offenses, the case will be forwarded to local juvenile probation officials. All juveniles arrested for an alleged delinquent offense which, if committed by an adult would be punishable by incarceration in a jail or prison are fingerprinted and their criminal history record entered into a statewide central information database.

The juvenile is then taken to the local **juvenile probation intake unit** where he/she goes through an intake process (see Schmalleger, pp.566-568) and is evaluated by an intake officer. Some cases may be resolved by counseling, others through referrals to other social agencies. In those cases where charges will be filed in court, the intake officer must decide where the juvenile will stay while awaiting judicial proceedings. Most are released to a parent or guardian but some are held in secure juvenile detention or in a shelter. Juvenile detention centers are operated by local juvenile probation departments or by private companies under contract. There are over 55 such centers in the state. Their function is to protect both the juvenile and the community and to ensure that the juvenile appears in court.

According to FC §54.01(e), a juvenile may only be detained if the court finds one of the following criteria present:

(1) he is likely to abscond or be removed from the jurisdiction of the court;

(2) suitable supervision, care, or protection for him is not being provided by a parent, guardian, custodian, or other person;
(3) he has no parent, guardian, custodian, or other person able to return him to the court when required;
(4) he may be dangerous to himself or may threaten the safety of the public if released; or
(5) he has previously been found to be a delinquent child or has previously been convicted of a penal offense punishable by a term in jail or prison and is likely to commit an offense if released.

If the juvenile is detained at intake, a judge must make a finding of probable cause within 48 hours and hold a **detention hearing** within one to two working days. The same criteria are used to determine whether the juvenile will be detained.

After charges are filed and while the juvenile is waiting to go to court, a probation officer begins a court investigation. This includes an assessment of the juvenile's behavior at home, at school, and in social relationships. The probation officer prepares a report to help the judge in making his/her decision.

In some cases, generally those involving younger offenders who committed less serious offenses, the juvenile will be diverted into a **deferred prosecution** program. This six-month program allows juveniles to avoid going through the adjudication process and limits their involvement with the formal juvenile justice system.

The court proceeding is known as an **adjudication hearing** (see Schmalleger, pp.568-569). The juvenile, his/her attorney, and members of his/her family appear before a judge or jury. Unlike some states, in Texas a juvenile has the right to a trial by jury unless the juvenile and his/her attorney waive that right. The jury verdict must be unanimous and, in determinate sentencing cases, there must be twelve jurors.

If the judge or jury determines that the juvenile committed a delinquent act, or some conduct that indicates a need for supervision, he/she is adjudicated for the offense and the judge will order a **disposition hearing** to determine the disposition of the juvenile (see Schmalleger, pp.569-572). There is no right to a jury in this stage, except in determinate sentencing cases. At the disposition hearing, the judge has a variety of options, ranging from dismissal of the case to long-term confinement. There are several basic dispositions used in juvenile court. If the juvenile committed a felony offense and is at least 14 years of age, the judge has the option of **certifying** the juvenile to stand trial in an adult criminal court. Juveniles who committed serious offenses may fall under the **Determinate Sentencing Law**, which allows the court to confine the juvenile for up to 40 years, first in a TYC facility and then later possibly in an adult institution. If the juvenile committed a less serious offense but still requires some type of confinement, the judge may order the juvenile committed to the TYC for a indeterminate period of time, although the juvenile will be automatically discharged upon reaching the age of 21. Finally, in most cases, the judge will place the juvenile on some type of probation involving supervision in the community (see Schmalleger, p.570) or in a residential treatment facility.

JUVENILE PROBATION IN TEXAS

Juvenile probation in Texas (see Schmalleger, p.570) is provided at the local and/or county level, by the 168 local juvenile probation departments. The **Texas Juvenile Probation Commission** collaborates with these local departments, providing funding and training; setting and enforcing minimum standards; and collecting, analyzing, and distributing relevant data.

Local juvenile probation departments handle approximately 97 percent of all juveniles who commit crimes in the state. Certification as a juvenile probation officer requires a bachelor's degree and one year of graduate study or one year of related work experience as well as 40 hours of basic probation training. There are over 2,000 certified juvenile probation officers in Texas. Each department is headed by a **Chief Juvenile Probation Officer** who is chosen by, and reports to, the County Juvenile Board. There are 168 Chief Juvenile Probation Officers who are responsible for the daily operations of the county department. In smaller counties, he/she may also supervise probationers.

THE TEXAS YOUTH COMMISSION

The **Texas Youth Commission** (TYC) is the juvenile corrections agency for the state of Texas. It was originally created in 1949 as the Texas Youth Development Council; the name was changed to the **Texas Youth Council** in 1957, and it was renamed the TYC in 1983. The TYC is responsible for the custody and rehabilitation of serious and chronic delinquents in the state. Its stated mission is "to protect the public, habilitate youth to become productive citizens, rehabilitate delinquent youth and help prevent delinquency."

Most juveniles committed to the TYC committed felony offenses when they were between the ages of ten and 17; the Commission has the option of maintaining jurisdiction over juvenile offenders until they reach age 21. In 1999, there were 2,979 new commitments to TYC. Of these, approximately 90 percent were male and 10 percent female. Approximately 25 percent were white, 33 percent were black, 42 percent were Hispanic, and 1 percent were of other races. Over 40 percent were committed for burglary (20 percent), drug offenses (11 percent), or simple assault (10 percent).

Approximately 80 percent of juveniles sent to TYC are assigned to one of the fifteen **secure correctional facilities** operated by TYC. In fiscal year 1999, the average daily population of these institutions was 4,047. This is an increase of 132 percent from 1995, when the average daily population was 1,744. The remainder (20 percent) are placed in **contract facilities** run by local governments and private sector providers. These include both residential facilities and non-residential programs and services. In 1999, the average daily population of juveniles in residential contract programs was 1,217. In addition, TYC operates nine **halfway houses**. After spending time in a secure facility, some juveniles are placed in a community-based halfway house as a transition back to the community. In 1999, the average daily population of TYC halfway houses was 212 juveniles.

If a juvenile commits a minor delinquent offense, the police may choose to simply warn the child and his/her parents. If the crime is more serious, the case will be referred to a county juvenile probation department and reviewed. Many cases are resolved through counseling and/or referrals. However, if the district attorney files charges against the juvenile, a probation officer will review the situation and report to the judge. In most cases, if the juvenile is adjudicated delinquent, the judge will order the youth placed either on probation supervision within the community or in a private residential treatment facility.

Only 3 percent of all juveniles referred to county juvenile probation departments are actually committed to the TYC. These are generally violent or chronic offenders. There are two ways in which juveniles may be committed to the TYC:

1. Juveniles who have committed extremely serious offenses may have been sentenced under Texas' Determinate Sentencing Law. This permits incarceration for up to 40 years; the sentence may be served first at TYC, with an optional court transfer to prison at a later date, depending on the juvenile's behavior.

2. Juveniles who have not received a determinate sentence may be sent to TYC for an indeterminate period. The amount of time is determined by TYC; offenders may remain in TYC custody until reaching the age of 21.

Although juveniles who are not committed to TYC under the Determinate Sentencing Law are assigned a minimum length of stay, this is merely the minimum time that they must spend in a residential program before being considered for parole. They are required to earn parole by showing progress in both rehabilitation and education programs and may stay well past their minimum length of stay. The average length of stay has been increasing steadily: in fiscal year 1995, the average length of stay was 9.1 months; in fiscal year 1999, this had increased to 12.8 months.

The minimum length of stay is determined by TYC, based on the juvenile's security classification. Juveniles without a determinate sentence are known as **Non-Sentenced Offenders** and may be classified as follows:

- **Type A Violent Offender**: a juvenile classified for committing or attempting to commit capital murder, murder, aggravated sexual assault, or sexual assault.

- **Type B Violent Offender**: a juvenile classified for committing or attempting to commit criminally negligent homicide, manslaughter, kidnapping, unlawful restraint, felony or aggravated assault, indecency with a child, injury to a child, elderly or disabled person, child abandonment or endangerment, felony deadly conduct, felony aiding suicide, first- or second-degree tampering with a consumer product, arson, robbery or aggravated robbery, burglary with intent to commit a violent offense, intoxication assault or manslaughter, participating in a riot at a TYC facility, or assault with bodily injury to TYC staff.

- **Chronic Serious Offender**: a juvenile who has been adjudicated on at least three separate occasions for committing a felony.

- **Controlled Substance Dealer**: a juvenile classified for felony-level drug manufacturing or delivery.

- **Firearms Offender**: a juvenile who had a firearm during the offense for which he/she has been classified.

- **General Offender**: includes all other juveniles, most of whom were are to TYC for non-violent or property crimes.

The minimum length of stay for Type A violent offenders is 24 months. The minimum length of stay for Type B violent offenders, chronic serious offenders, controlled substance dealers, and firearms offenders is 12 months. The minimum length of stay for general offenders is 9 months.

All juveniles committed to TYC are first sent to the **Marlin Orientation and Assessment Center** where they undergo a medical examination, psychological evaluation, education assessment, social summary, a needs assessment to determine requirements for specialized treatment, and an orientation to the TYC program and expectations. These evaluations and tests are used to determine where the juvenile will be placed.

Most juveniles generally spend most of their minimum length of stay in a secure residential facility. As they near the end of this period, they may be moved to a halfway house or residential contract program, or may remain in the secure facility until release on parole. Juveniles placed on parole receive supervision from a parole officer. A juvenile who performs well while on parole will be discharged from the TYC. In addition, TYC authority ends when the juvenile reaches the age of 21; at this point, discharge is automatic. Juveniles who commit additional criminal offenses while under TYC jurisdiction may be charged as adults. Juveniles with a determinate sentence will be assigned to a secure residential facility and may be transferred to the Texas Department of Criminal Justice at a later date.

TYC rehabilitation is based on a concept known as **resocialization**, which focuses on correctional therapy, education, work, and discipline training. Juveniles spend 16 hours a day involved in various resocialization activities. These are divided into phases through which each juvenile may move through at his/her own pace; he/she must show specific competencies in each phase before moving on to the next. Basic needs such as food, clothing, shelter, medical care, and due process are provided to all juveniles in TYC custody. However, juveniles earn privileges and rewards by completing resocialization phases and complying with TYC program rules.

In addition to resocialization, TYC provides specialized intensive treatment for juveniles with identified special needs. These programs include those designed for capital offenders, sex offenders, juveniles with chemical dependencies, severely emotionally disturbed juveniles, and mentally retarded juveniles. The assessment process at the Marlin Center is designed to identify juveniles who will most benefit from specialized treatment and to place them in the appropriate program.

JUVENILE PAROLE IN TEXAS

The TYC is also responsible for supervising juveniles who are released into the community on **parole**. The TYC Parole Program includes two main components: **Parole Core Services** and **Parole Management**.

Parole Core Services includes surveillance, resocialization, and sanctions. It emphasizes juvenile participation in education, vocational training, employment, treatment, counseling, and community services; juveniles are required to spend at least 40 hours per week in such constructive activities. There are three primary levels of parole supervision: intensive, moderate, and minimum. Juveniles move to a less restrictive level of supervision based on performance, including compliance with parole conditions and how well they meet individual case planning objectives. To qualify for release from parole, a juvenile must be at the minimum level of parole supervision. Sanctions occur if juveniles violate parole program conditions or expectations. Parole Management involves identifying, gathering, and analyzing data on juvenile parole in Texas and compiling reports for program evaluation and review.

Juveniles who are granted parole must agree to a number of conditions of supervision. These include:

- must obey all federal, state, county, and city laws and ordinances
- must report any arrests or violations of the law (including minor citations) to his/her parole officer within five days
- may not change approved placement, leave the county of placement for more than 24 hours, or leave the state of Texas without the permission of his/her parole officer
- must notify his/her parole officer prior to any change of residence
- will not cause physical pain or bodily injury to any person (including him/herself)
- will not own, use, sell, or have in his/her control any deadly weapon, firearm, explosive devices, or ammunition
- will not use any controlled substance, alcohol, or intoxicant
- will submit to drug screening tests as instructed by his/her parole officer
- will not associate with anyone who is using or is in possession of a controlled substance, alcohol, intoxicant, drug paraphernalia, or weapon
- will not intentionally damage or destroy property
- will not associate with gang members or participate in gang activity
- will follow all instructions given by his/her parole officer and agree to meet all expectations outlined in the individual plan of supervision

All juveniles classified as sentenced offenders (e.g., those with determinate sentences) and those classified as Violent A must remain in the parole program until reaching the age of 21. For other juveniles, successful completion of the parole program requires him/her to:

- meet his/her minimum length of stay
- meet all objects of his/her individual case plan
- achieve three consecutive months (90 days) of 40-hour constructive activity weeks
- complete all required community service hours
- achieve the minimum level of surveillance
- achieve a designed success plan
- develop an effective and attainable discharge plan

CHAPTER 10

DRUGS AND CRIME IN TEXAS

THE DRUG PROBLEM IN TEXAS

Schmalleger devotes Chapter 15 to a discussion of the drug problem in the United States. **Drug abuse** is a serious problem in Texas, as in most states. Approximately 2.6 million adults and 200,000 juveniles in Texas have problems with alcohol or drugs. Illicit drugs enter the state from Mexico through a number of Texas cities, including El Paso, Laredo, and Brownsville, along with many smaller border towns; the drugs then move north for distribution through Houston and Dallas/Fort Worth. Dugs also move eastward from San Diego through Lubbock and from El Paso to Amarillo and Dallas/Fort Worth. Heroin and cocaine are imported into the country through Texas seaports and through the international airports in Houston and Dallas/Fort Worth.

Cocaine and Crack

In 1998, there were a total of 374 deaths in Texas that included a mention of cocaine (see Schmalleger, pp.598-599). This number has been increasing since 1995. In 1998, the average age of those who died cocaine-related deaths was almost 37 years. Of these, 48 percent were white, 30 percent were black, and 21 percent were Hispanic. Crack cocaine is the primary illicit drug that is abused by adult clients who are admitted to publicly funded treatment programs in Texas. Approximately two-thirds of all cases are male.

According to the DEA, cocaine is easily obtainable in Texas at both the wholesale and retail levels. In the Houston area, powder cocaine sells for $9,500 to $14,000 per kilogram wholesale and $14,000 to $18,000 per kilogram retail. The price is higher in northern Texas. In 1999, the price of powder ranged between $500 and $1,200 per ounce and $50 to $275 per gram. The price of an ounce of crack cocain ranged from $500 to $1,000 whereas a rock cost between $10 and $20.

Heroin

In 1998, there were 374 deaths that included a mention of heroin or narcotics (see Schmalleger, pp.600-601). As with cocaine and crack, this number has been increasing steadily since 1995. The average age of those dying heroin-related deaths was approximately 37 years, a decrease from the previous year, showing an increase in overdose deaths among younger persons.

Heroin is the third most common drug (after alcohol and crack cocain) for which adult clients are admitted to state-funded substance abuse treatment programs. Most addicts inject heroin, although a small percentage inhale the drug.

The most commonly used form of heroin is Texas is black tar. Currently, this type of heroin has a street price of $10 to $20 per capsule, $120 to $300 per gram, $700 to $5,000 per ounce, and $62,000 to $175,000 per kilogram. Other types of heroin used in Texas include Mexican brown heroin, which sells for $900 to $3,500 per ounce; Southeast Asian heroin, which costs $3,500 to $5,50 per ounce and $150,000 to $175,000 per kilogram; Southwest Asian heroin, which sells for $85,000 per kilogram; and Colombian heroin, which costs $1,000 per gram.

Alcohol

The most commonly abused drug in Texas is alcohol (see Schmalleger, pp.585-587). The rate of direct alcohol deaths (those in which alcohol or drugs caused the death) has remained stable since 1994; however, the rate of indirect alcohol deaths (in which alcohol or drugs did not cause the death but were involved, such as violent crime or car accidents) have been increasing. More individuals in Texas are arrested for DWI and public intoxication than for any other substance abuse offenses.

Marijuana

Marijuana (see Schmalleger, pp.597-598) is the primary problem for 9 percent of all adults admitted to state-funded treatment programs in 1999. The average age of clients with marijuana problems has increased from 24 in 1985 to 27 in 1999. The proportion of juveniles admitted for marijuana abuse has increased from 35 percent in 1987 to 74 percent in 1999.

According to the DEA, marijuana is readily available throughout Texas, although large seizures of the drug (up to multiple tons) are common. Prices depend on qualify, quantity, demand, and availability. In southern Texas, a pound of marijuana costs $500 to $850 per pound wholesale; in the northern part of the state, the price is $400 to $700 per pound. An ounce of marijuana sells for $35 to $60.

Drug Abuse among Juveniles

In 1998, the **Texas School Survey of Substance Abuse Among Students** surveyed over 150,000 students in grades seven through 12 regarding their use of tobacco, alcohol, inhalants, and various illicit drugs. The study found that current (within the past month) use of tobacco among older students is increasing, alcohol use has remained stable but high, the use of inhalants has increased among all students, and the use of illegal drugs has increased among older students.

The most commonly used substances by juveniles in Texas were alcohol, tobacco, marijuana, inhalants, and cocaine (which replaced uppers). Approximately 58 percent of Texas students used some substance during the past school year while 76 percent reported some use during their lifetime. Although students in the lower grades were much more likely to use inhalants, all other substances were more commonly used by students in the upper grades.

According to the Texas Commission on Alcohol and Drug Abuse, approximately 59 percent of juveniles in the custody of the Texas Youth Commission are chemically dependent. An additional 15 percent abuse alcohol and/or drugs in some way.

Drug Use among Offenders

A state-run survey of 782 male prisoners in the Texas Department of Criminal Justice Institutional Division found that 86 percent admitted to using an illegal drug in their lifetime. Approximately 36 percent had used an illegal drug in their last month on the street. The survey also found that inmates were almost twice as likely as non-incarcerated men in Texas to abuse or be dependant upon alcohol and were about six times as likely to abuse or be dependant on other drugs. They were more than five times more likely to have used powder cocaine and 18 times more likely to have used heroin than non-incarcerated men in Texas. Approximately 46 percent of male inmates required treatment for a substance dependency upon entering prison.

THE TEXAS COMMISSION ON ALCOHOL AND DRUG ABUSE

Originally, the Texas legislature separated the problems of alcohol and drug abuse by creating separate agencies to deal with each problem In 1953 the legislature created the **Texas Commission on Alcoholism** (TCA). Although its original purpose was limited to distributing public information about alcoholism, the agency's responsibilities soon expanded and it became the primary authority on alcoholism for the state. In 1970, the governor created the **State Program on Drug Abuse**, which later became the **Drug Abuse Prevention Division** (DAPD) of the Texas Department of Community Affairs. DAPD was the state agency responsible for coordinating drug abuse programs and administering federal funds for drug abuse.

In 1985, the legislature merged the TCA and the DAPD to create the **Texas Commission on Alcohol and Drug Abuse** (TCADA). The purpose of the TCADA is to address serious substance abuse issues affecting Texas residents. The Commission is made up of six members who are appointed by the state governor with the advice and consent of the Senate. At least three of the members must have experience in activities such as business management, financial management, auditing, contract management, etc. Members of the TCADA serve staggered terms of six years.

Section 461.001 of the Texas Health and Safety Code (HSC) outlines the policy of the TCADA:

> Chemical dependency is a preventable and treatable illness and public health problem affecting the general welfare and the economy of the state. The legislature recognizes the need for proper and sufficient facilities, programs, and procedures for prevention, intervention, treatment, and rehabilitation. It is the policy of this state that a chemically dependent person shall be offered a continuum of services that will enable the person to lead a normal life as a productive member of society.

The TCADA contracts with public and private agencies to provide services for the prevention and treatment of substance abuse in Texas. Currently, TCADA has contracts with over 200 agencies; it has also licensed approximately 5,500 chemical dependency counselors and 820 treatment sites, as well as certifying programs for drug offenders, alcohol awareness for minors, and DWI education. Essentially, it provides for the delivery of services for substance abuse prevention, intervention, and treatment.

In 1997, TCADA also established eleven **Prevention Resource Centers** throughout the state. Their function is to emphasize the importance of prevention through education; facilitate the dissemination of prevention information regarding alcohol, tobacco, and other drugs; and coordinate substance abuse prevention efforts.

The TCADA has three major service functions. **Prevention** involves stopping the onset of illegal substance abuse and encouraging drug-free lifestyles. **Intervention** focuses on interrupting the illegal use of substances and breaking the cycle of harmful substance use. **Treatment** involves assisting an individual to become chemical free and to remain free of illegal substances. All three functions involve multiple strategies.

TCADA is divided into four main branches. The **Finance and Administration Branch** deals with budget and fiscal services, information technology, administrative support services, and human resources. The **Licensing and Enforcement Branch** deals with regulatory functions and agency compliance. The **Program Branch** is responsible for providing direction in program planning and evaluation, program management, and program development. Finally, the **General Counsel** is responsible for overseeing legal support, communications, and public information.

TEXAS DRUG TREATMENT COURTS

Texas, like most other states, has developed treatment-based drug courts (see Schmalleger, pp.611-612). A drug court is a special court which handles cases involving drug-addicted offenders through the use of extensive supervision and treatment. The court also increases the coordination of various agencies and resources available to drug abusers, increasing the cost-effectiveness of the programs and providing the offender with access to a wide variety of programs and resources. The concept involves treating drug addicts in the criminal justice system, rather than placing them in prison or on probation. In Texas, it costs approximately $3,000 per year to place an offender in a drug court program. This is two to three times more expensive than placing the offender on regular probation, but significantly less expensive than placing the offender in a secure prison facility.

The Travis County Drug Court

The **Travis County Drug Court** is known as the **SHORT** (the System of Healthy Options for Release and Transition) Court. Located in Austin, it is a diversion program for those offenders who meet the following criteria:

- arrested for felony-level possession of a controlled substance
- have no prior convictions for violent offenses
- have no other charges pending

SHORT is designed to provide opportunities for rehabilitation and is an alternative to traditional criminal processing. Participants waive their right to a trial and agree to obey the judge's orders, giving the judge more freedom in requiring them to go through counseling, in-patient drug treatment, etc.

The program lasts for one year (52 weeks) and includes heavy supervision, frequent drug screening (e.g., urinalysis), counseling (e.g., twelve-step meetings), school or job training, and participation in substance abuse treatment and education programs, and provides various support services for offenders. Each participant is assigned a primary counselor who assists him/her in completing the program. The SHORT judge is also active in developing case plans, providing treatment referrals, and handing down court sanctions. If a program participant tests negative for drugs and attends the requirement meetings and treatment programs for a prescribed period of time, the treatment plan will be modified by reducing the requirements (e.g., placing the offender on a lighter level of supervision).

If an offender successfully completes the SHORT program, remaining drug free for a court-specified period of time, the criminal charges against him/her will be dismissed. Offenders who resume using drugs or who fail to make adequate progress through the program may be moved back to a higher level of supervision; ordered to attend more counseling sessions or undergo more frequent drug testing; required to participate in a residential treatment program; or even be sent to jail for a period of time. Offenders who continue to abuse drugs may be returned to the court to face their original drug charge(s).

Between August, 1993, and May, 2000, the drug court handled 940 offenders. Of these, 489 were successfully diverted from the criminal courts, 227 are currently enrolled in and participating in the program, and 219 were unsuccessfully discharged. Five offenders died while in the program. Between 1993 and 1997, 16 percent of the drug court graduates were rearrested. Only 3 percent were convicted.

APPENDIX A

WEB SITES OF INTEREST

There is a large amount of information on Texas and the Texas criminal justice system available on the worldwide web. Below is a selection of web sites that may be of interest to students.

GENERAL TEXAS WEB SITES:

http://www.state.tx.us/

The State of Texas home page with information on Texas government, economy, education, health care, crime and much more. Links to a variety of state government agencies may be found on this site.

http://www.governor.state.tx.us/

The home page for the Office of the Governor of Texas.

http://www.senate.state.tx.us/

The home page for the Texas State Senate.

http://www.house.state.tx.us/

The home page for the Texas House of Representatives.

http://www.oag.state.tx.us/

This is the home page for the Attorney General of Texas.

http://www.tsl.state.tx.us/

The home page of the Texas State Library and Archives.

http://www.texasbar.com/pubinf/legalinfo/cjp.htm

This web site includes a variety of information on the criminal justice process in Texas.

LEGAL INFORMATION:

http://www.capitol.state.tx.us/txconst/toc.html

The Constitution of the State of Texas is available on the Internet.

http://www.capitol.state.tx.us/statutes/statutes.html

Texas state statutes are available on the world wide web. Statutes of interest include the Penal Code, the Code of Criminal Procedure, and the Family Code.

http://info.sos.state.tx.us/pub/plsql/readtac$ext.viewtac

The Texas Administrative Code includes information on both public safety and corrections.

TEXAS POLICE-RELATED WEB SITES:

http://www.txdps.state.tx.us/
The Texas Department of Public Safety home page.

http://www.ci.houston.tx.us/departme/police/home.htm
The home page of the Houston Police Department.

http://co.jefferson.tx.us/sheriff/mission.htm
The Jefferson County Sheriff's Office home page.

http://www.co.harris.tx.us/so/
The Harris County Sheriff's Office home page.

http://www.ci.dallas.tx.us/dpd/
The home page of the Dallas Police Department.

http://www.tcleose.state.tx.us/
The home page of the Texas Commission on Law Enforcement Officer Standards and Education.

http://www.tdprs.state.tx.us/
The home page of the Texas Department of Protective and Regulatory Services.

http://www.ci.austin.tx.us/police
The Austin Police Department home page.

http://www.ci.huntsville.tx.us/
The City of Huntsville Police Department home page.

http://www.ci.sat.tx.us/sapd
The San Antonio Police Department home page.

http://www.ci.corpus-christi.tx.us/services/police/index.htm
The Corpus Christi Police Department home page.

http://rgfn.epcc.edu/users/eppd/police.htm
The El Paso Police Department home page.

http://www.irvingpd.com
The Irving Police Department home page.

http://www.utexas.edu/admin/utpd
The University of Texas at Austin Police Department web page.

http://www.victexpolice.org

The Victoria Police Department home page.

TEXAS COURT SYSTEM INFORMATION:

http://www.courts.state.tx.us/

The home page for the Texas Judiciary. This page includes links to all the main types of courts in the state as well as many other court-related links.

http://www.oca.courts.state.tx.us/

The home page of the Texas Office of Court Administration.

http://www.weblocator.com/attorney/tx/law/c03.html#txc030200

This web site outlines the criminal process in Texas.

http://www.state.tx.us/agency/242.html

This web page provides information on the Texas Commission on Judicial Conduct.

INFORMATION ON CORRECTIONS IN TEXAS:

http://www.tdcj.state.tx.us/index.htm

The home page of the Texas Department of Criminal Justice.

http://tdcj.state.tx.us/bpp/index.html

The home page of the Texas Board of Pardons and Paroles.

http://www.tjcs.state.tx.us

The home page of the Texas Commission on Jail Standards.

http://www.tdcj.state.tx.us/statistics/stats-home.htm

This web page provides statistics on the use of the death penalty in Texas.

http://www.lonestar.texas.net/~acohen/tcadp/

This is the web site of the Texas Coalition to Abolish the Death Penalty.

JUVENILE JUSTICE AND DRUG-RELATED WEB SITES:

http://www.tyc.state.tx.us/index.html

The home page of the Texas Youth Commission.

http://www.tjpc.state.tx.us/

The Texas Juvenile Probation Commission web site.

http://www.dhs.state.tx.us/

The home page of the Texas Department of Human Services.

http://www.acf.dhhs.gov/

The home page of the Texas Department of Health and Human Services - The Administration for Children and Families.

http://www.tcada.state.tx.us/

The Texas Commission on Alcohol and Drug Abuse web site.

APPENDIX B

INTERVIEWS

An Interview with D.C. "Jim" Dozier, Executive Director Texas Commission on Law Enforcement Standards and Education Austin, Texas

D.C. "Jim" Dozier has been the executive director of TCLEOSE since September 1, 1994. Jim Dozier has a Ph.D. from the University of Texas in behavioral science, a law degree from South Texas College of Law, a masters degree in education, and a bachelors degree in criminal justice.

Dr. Dozier began his career in law enforcement with the Houston Police Department in 1967 at the age of 19. He became a police officer to help his mother support their family. The salary of $110 per week was very appealing to Jim. The Houston Police Academy was 16 weeks long. Upon academy graduation, new officers were assigned with an experienced officer, but there was no formal FTO program. Jim Dozier as a new officer was assigned to the four police stations for one month each. The concept was to expose the officer to the various types of persons, personalities, and cultures throughout Houston.

Cultural diversity was not taught in the academy but learned by hands-on experience. "A new officer learned by watching and imitating the actions of the experienced officer. Force was always met with force," Dozier said.

Jim Dozier's first police assignment was in the high crime area of Houston called Sunnyside. "In 1967 there was not much sophistication in the police department, no walkie talkies, no air conditioning in the patrol cars. Policing in 1967 was physical policing," recalls Dozier.

After five years with the Houston Police Department, Dr. Dozier obtained a position with the U.S. Customs Department Internal Affairs Division. In 1973 the Drug Enforcement Administration was established from four divisions in three federal agencies which combated the drug problem, Bureau of Narcotics and Dangerous Drugs, Narcotics Advance Research Team, Officer of National Drug Intelligence, Office of Drug Abuse Law Enforcement, and U.S. Customs Drug Investigations Division. Jim Dozier became a DEA Special Agent assigned in Houston as a result of this merger. He worked undercover and had several special assignments throughout the U.S.

As executive director of TCLEOSE, Jim Dozier's duties include implementing the philosophy and policies of the Commissioners. Dr. Dozier suggests policies to the Commissioners and manages the agency as it follows the requirements set forth by the legislature and the recommendations of specially appointed subcommittees.

Jim Dozier sees new officers today having to deal with conflicting and ambiguous roles. "The officers must work crazy hours, and receive a modest salary. Many of these officers have new families and new financial responsibilities such as a house mortgage. The new officers need to understand the social difficulties of policing and their impact on the officers' families. The new officers should be taught the stressors of police work and how they can affect the family life during their initial training. Police officers are called to conflict resolutions but they are not always taught how to address the same conflicts at home. It is very important for the officer to know how to transition from police officer to family member," Dozier says.

"The police officer is a role model. The police officer must realize he/she is a part of society not apart from society. TCLEOSE has established public service awards for Texas police officers. TCLEOSE wants police officers who are good citizens to receive his/her due recognition. This statewide recognition is intended to illustrate that the men and women in law enforcement are not the stereotypical officers portrayed in the entertainment industry.

"Texas is a national leader in recognizing domestic disturbance issues and developing programs to address those problems. The state legislature has made the fact very clear: a police officer must make an arrest when there is an assault in a domestic disturbance," Dr. Dozier points out. "When a weak person is abused, all of society suffers."

"Training in anti-terrorism is being directed by the federal government. Texas follows the lead of the federal government for this training. Texas A&M has a project to study weapons of mass destruction. Terrorist training is mainly concentrated in the large urban centers. Terrorists will destroy something that will make international news in order to bring attention to their cause. Terrorists most likely will not attack a small rural area. But all Texas law enforcement officers need to be aware of terrorists. Texas with its massive border with Mexico is an inviting target. All police officers need to be trained on how to identify potential terrorists as they transverse Texas. A simple traffic stop ultimately was identified as the Oklahoma City bomber. As the world becomes smaller, all officers must be aware of the terrorist problem.

"Fighting the drug problem will always be controversial. Which is most effective, law enforcement or rehabilitation? The core of the problem is that the two sides of the issue do not want to listen to the opposing viewpoint. A pastor at a church once said during a sermon, 'The trouble with a person that has all the answers is that they do not leave any room for questions.' Society needs to look at alternative strategies in fighting drugs. Texas has trained more officers to be drug recognition experts than any other state in the nation.

"A serious problem with drugs is the propensity for violence. Police officers should be trained to be aware that violence can occur when drugs are involved. Officers should conduct good aggressive police work in fighting drugs, but they should never stereotype any group of people to be more inclined to possess or sell drugs. Training in human awareness and understanding will help the officers conduct legal and ethical drug investigations.

"The concept of community policing is not new. I would consider community policing as a 'back to the future' concept. In 1968 I walked a beat in Houston and I knew everyone and they knew me. Back then it was called police-community relations. Today, the difference is community policing is better integrated into the entire police effort. Community policing refines what had always been done into a more coordinated effort and the results are better communicated to all of the officers.

"There are many innovations at the Commission I am proud of. But currently the top three would be: One, all legislatively required in-service courses for police officers be available over the Internet at no cost to the officer or the police department.

"Two, all training records can be sent to TCLEOSE electronically. Law enforcement agencies no longer have to send their records to TCLEOSE through the mail and then have the data entered into our computer system by one of our staff. The information can go directly into our system by the reporting agency. This reduces the chance of errors, eliminates duplication of effort, ensures that all law enforcement officers are current with their required training, and credits those officers who have advanced with formal or specialized training.

"Three, TCLEOSE will continue to encourage college education for all law enforcement officers. All agencies should require some type of college degree. I am not saying all officers should have a criminal justice degree, but there should be flexibility so agencies can receive new officers that have diverse backgrounds and education. The law enforcement has been trying for years to be considered a professional career. National accreditation goes a long way in achieving that professional level. But when agencies do not require some type of advanced education as a pre-requisite to employment, law enforcement will become a semi-professional career.

"Discretion must be given to police officers. But TCLEOSE cannot effectively mandate a specific class on how to use discretion. As officers become better trained and formally educated, they will use their discretion more wisely. Highly trained, professional, ethical police officers will do the right thing when they must use discretion.

"Although law enforcement is still a male dominated career, there are very important roles for women. The use of women in all aspects of law enforcement have been a tremendous success, much more than some of the most liberal or innovative police administrators 20 years ago would ever imagine. Men and women have various strengths, and both groups have valuable and critical roles to play in law enforcement.

"As an administrator I want the best persons for the job regardless of gender, race, age. An administrator must be open to accept all persons who are capable of performing the job and 'play the best players.' If the best players are women, or persons of another race, that should not influence the decision making process.

"It has been proven that college education along with training in the use of force will reduce the officers' number of occasions that they will use force against the citizenry. Officers are trained in the proper escalation of force, the force continuum. Texas does an excellent job in training its police officers regarding the legal and practical issues associated with the use of force. The training emphasizes safety for society and the officers while also considering cultural diversity.

"The recent violence in our schools nationwide is a social problem, a problem directly connected to problems in some families. In Texas the state legislature appropriates money to each police department for specialized training. There are specialized training programs for local police departments and school district police to better identify children who may be more inclined to violence. This allows for early intervention before violence occurs. Emphasis is on communication with the child, the family, and counseling for all participants.

"Emergency telecommunications has specific required training. This finally allows telecommunicators (dispatchers) to have a career track and recognition of their importance. The telecommunicators are important linkages between the officers and the initial public request for service.

"Accomplishments at the Commission I am most proud of are the advancement of professional training for police officers, jailers, and emergency telecommunicators. The advancement has been in every area that the Commission on Law Enforcement oversees, not just law enforcement, but also jailers, telecommunicators, and crime lab technicians. I am also very proud that the Commission worked with the Fleetwood Foundation and others to have a Texas Peace Officers Memorial built in Austin. The memorial remembers officers who have lost their lives while performing their enforcement duties.

"I am proud of the law enforcement profession. Being a police officer is an affair of the heart, not the pocketbook. A person must be happy with their career regardless of the salary. Life is too short to hate your job. Being a police officer you are able to have a noticeable impact on society. I am very happy to see eager young talent from a variety of backgrounds enter this profession. When these young people work in the criminal justice system they will be able to recall the number of lives they influenced and impacted."

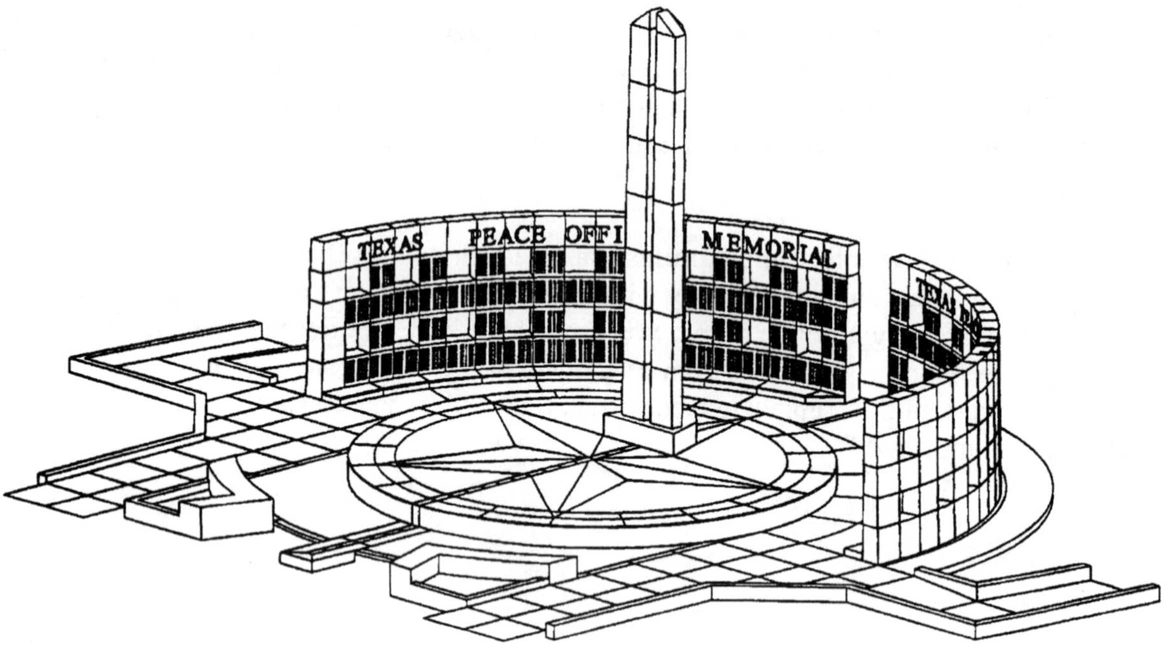

Texas Peace Officers' Memorial

An Interview with
Timothy A. Braaten, Chief of Police
Victoria Police Department
Victoria, Texas

Chief Timothy Braaten has been in law enforcement since July 1968 starting with the Detroit Police Department as a police officer at Wayne State University. Timothy Braaten attended a 12-week training academy prior to his assignment at Wayne State. Upon graduation he was assigned to a field training program for about eight weeks. Tim Braaten says his Field Training Officer (FTO), John Mc Auliffe, was an excellent FTO and trainer.

After five years Tim Braaten went to the Saginaw, Michigan, Police Department to work in the Planning and Research Division. He served as deputy chief of police in Grand Haven, Michigan, from 1976 to 1980. From 1980 to 1983, Tim Braaten was chief of police in Mequon, Michigan. Braaten took over the job after the previous chief was shot and killed on duty.

Tim Braaten was an assistant general agent for a short period of time in 1984 and made a good salary. But his passion for justice lead him to accept a position as Chief of Police at Oak Ridge, Tennessee. In 1993 Tim Braaten accepted the chief of police position in Victoria, Texas.

"Police are called to order maintenance issues and public nuisances by the community. The public judges the amount of crime in the community by the number of minor crimes and nuisances there are. The police sometimes mistakenly believe that the community is more interested in Part I crimes. The police will tell the community that crime is down by so much of a percentage. Police will emphasis the numbers. This is not the case. The public gets bored listening to the numbers. Only about 20% of the Part I crimes committed in Victoria are stranger on stranger. Last year of the 30 sexual assaults reported in Victoria, 18 were committed by acquaintances, 2 by relatives, and 10 by strangers. The public wants to feel safe in their neighborhood and when they go to work or to the store, and to feel that their children are safe. Often at community meetings with the police, the public is more interested in controlling loud noises, speeding cars on their neighborhood streets, or loitering than the number of Part I crimes. The police can shape the image of crime by listening to and addressing the community's concern about specific law violations. The police should educate the public about crime in the community and what they can do to reduce their risk of exposure.

"In Victoria, the patrol officers' time is spent on: 20% order maintenance, 45% service, 25% law enforcement, 10% crime prevention.

"There are 105 commissioned officers and supervisors with the Victoria Police Department. The department has six female officers, one of whom is a lieutenant and a shift commander. There are four sergeants who are from a minority group.

"Victoria Police Department has been successful recently in recruiting minorities and women because the department has shown it will make available to women and minorities the same career opportunities that white males receive. When members of the minority community and women see that they have the same opportunities, they apply in large numbers. In the last promotion board for sergeant, the top four candidates were Hispanic."

Chief Braaten was presented with Susan E. Martin's ***Female Officers on the Move? A Status Report of Women in Policing***, which stated, "Women [officers] pose a threat to work group solidarity by penetrating the emotional masks men wear and inhibiting their use of 'raunchy language.'" He was asked whether he felt this was an accurate statement concerning the sexual harassment of women in policing.

Chief Braaten disagreed with the statement. "There is an intensive emphasis to have a professional organization and that means no tolerance for sexual harassment. One of the best compliments a woman officer can receive is that she is a good cop. When a female officer does a good job, occasionally male officers might forget the gender difference and make a statement, though not directed to harass or defile, that is inappropriate to any group in a professional organization.

"Women in law enforcement have made a significant difference. Women are very good at containment skills as opposed to men who generally use confrontational skills. Women will contain and wait for backup, they will confront only when necessary to their safety or the community. Women are better report writers, have better memories, and they can tell when someone is lying more often than men. They have more strength of mind. In a confrontation, women will use pressure points rather than strength or a boxing match.

"The opportunities have opened completely since I started in law enforcement. Women did not participate in physical training in the police academy I went through in Detroit. As time progressed, more opportunities opened for minorities and women and that increased their desire to enter law enforcement.

"James Q Wilson's style of policing which best represents Victoria Police Department is service style with the legalistic style used when necessary.

"Victoria Police department uses decoys for buying drugs. The department works hard to make arrest of persons who sell drugs. Most police departments have a challenge in fighting drugs. The communities will not tolerate drug dealing occurring on city streets. When enforcement is strict and swift, drug dealing goes indoors and this is much more difficult to enforce. The department also uses decoys to enforce prostitution laws.

"Officers utilize traffic enforcement as a means of crime abatement. The department has a hostage negotiating team and a sex crime unit which investigates sex crimes against adults and children. The department does not have a repeat offenders unit but a close watch is kept on what are referred to as the predators, those that commit multiple crimes.

"The department's procedure for handling bomb threats is to make all possible efforts to prevent the detonation of the explosive. Safety of the citizens and officers is the primary concern. When an emergency telecommunications operator receives a call about a bomb, a unit will be assigned the call using a special radio code. All communications after that are by telephone. Portable communication radios are prohibited at the scene. If the bomb has not detonated, the Victoria Police Department has jurisdiction. The Victoria Fire Department Arson Division has investigatory responsibility, with the cooperation of the police department. If a suspected explosive device is found, the officer in charge will immediately order an evacuation of the building and area. If the device is found in a federal building, the FBI and ATF are notified.

"The department integrates community oriented policing within its day-to-day operations. An officer may submit a problem oriented policing (P.O.P) request to his supervisor. The officer, with guidance of the supervisor, coordinates and works on the P.O.P. with others in his/her beat. The initiating officer is responsible to come up with an answer for the problem. An example of a POP file is found on pp.130-134 of this Supplement.

"The discretion of police officers is tremendous but there are department guidelines which are a requirement of accreditation. For example, every use of force will be documented and reviewed by the chief of police. This immediate review of the officers' actions limits the use of discretion. Guidelines are generally found on any high risk operations such as vehicle pursuit and the use of force. All officers are expected to know all high risk department directives by heart.

"Victoria Police Department has a pursuit policy. Every pursuit will be reported and an immediate review of the pursuit will be conducted by the shift commander at the scene. Roadblocks are prohibited without the express permission of the chief of police or designee. It is preferred to drop off of a pursuit rather than risk injury. Officers are prohibited from harassing an officer who drops off from a pursuit. Harassing officers would receive days off without pay.

"In the six years I have been here, there hasn't been a use of deadly force. Rubber projectiles are used, rather than deadly force, when there is the opportunity . All officers review the deadly force policy each time they re-qualify with their handgun. Officers are expected to follow seven levels of the continuum of force.

"There are 16 street gangs and four prison gangs in Victoria. The prison gangs are involved in most of the gang style killings. Officers watch and listen to the gang leadership to determine what illegal activities are being planned.

"In combating the drug problem the department will do everything possible as long as it is legal. The department has a lieutenant and four undercover officers who will buy drugs. The officers will then document their activities and obtain grand jury indictments of the drug dealers. The department works closely with the Victoria Sheriff's Office, DEA, and any other agency which can assist in the enforcement of controlled substance laws.

"The best way to combat police corruption is to have multiple people doing the same job, career rotation. Keep more than one person involved in cases. Do not isolate a group or division of officers. Officers will also assess the risk of corruption. They will determine if the risk and the actual punishment are greater than the rewards of the corruption.

TO: All 100 Zone Officers

REFERENCE: POP File

FROM: Officer Townsend *#5105*

I have been contacted by several neighbors reference the Prostitution and drug activity occurring at the above address. Neighbors are frightened of the individuals involved and request to remain anonymous for fear of retaliation. I contacted the owner of the property, XXXXX Brazoria Tx. 77422, who stated that he was unaware of the problems we have had at the location and stated he would cooperate with us in any action necessary to clean up the location. I contacted the renter at the location, XXXXX B/M XXXXX at XXXXX, who stated that he will cooperate with VPD.

A check of the CAD revealed 96 calls for service or contacts from 01/01/99 to the present, at 500 blk of XXXXX, 600 blk of XXXXX, and 700 blk of XXXXX. The majority of the activity in this area emanates from XXXXX.

The property of XXXXX and XXXXX are both owned by XXXXX XXXXX. XXXXX XXXXX rents the rear apartment which is not attached to the house. The house is vacant. XXXXX stated that he would press charges on trespassers in and around the apartment he resides in. XXXXX stated that he would also press charges on individuals on the property at XXXXX. I have received a FAX from XXXXX XXXXX stating he would press charges on anyone on that property other than XXXXX XXXXX and XXXXX XXXXX who picks up rent from XXXXX. No Trespassing Signs have been posted on the property, in plain view. Two in the front of XXXXX and one at XXXXX.. XXXXX stated he will sign a statement stating he will also press charges on all unwanted individual on XXXXX.

Further investigation pending the results of this action.

PRIOR INCIDENTS AT '700 Block

1.	99-08639	09/18/99	TRAFFIC STOP
2.	6624239523	09/10/99	OS-ON SCENE
3	9060352	09/02/99	OS-ON SCENE
4	9056709	08/17/99	OUT WITH B/F
5	9042049	06/16/99	OUT W/HM
6	9041374	06/14/99	TRAFFIC STOP
7	9033341	05/15/99	TRAFFIC STOP
8	9031384	05/07/99	TRAFFIC STOP
9	9031117	05/06/99	TRAFFIC STOP
10	9023465	04/05/99	TRAFFIC STOP
11	9020621	03/24/99	TRAFFIC STOP
12	9018144	03/15/99	OUT WITH H/F
13	9016689	03/09/99	W/HF
14	9013631	02/24/99	TRAFFIC STOP
15	9008470	02/05/99	TRAFFIC STOP
16	9002289	01/13/99	OS-ON SCENE
17	9000820	01/07/99	TRAFFIC STOP
18	8078117	11/09/98	TRAFFIC STOP
19	8075146	10/28/98	TRAFFIC STOP

PRIOR INCIDENTS AT '600 Block

1.	7746459878	11/10/99	OUT WITH B/M
2.	99-08243	11/02/99	TRAFFIC STOP
3	9074218	10/31/99	TRAFFIC STOP
4	9074215	10/31/99	OS-ON SCENE
5	9073115	10/27/99	OS-ON SCENE
6	9072023	10/22/99	OS-ON SCENE
7	9058610	08/25/99	OS-ON SCENE
8	9058212	08/24/99	WITH SUBJECT
9	9055889	08/13/99	TRAFFIC STOP
10	9053949	08/05/99	TRAFFIC STOP
11	9052771	07/31/99	FEMALE SUBJ
12	9021230	03/26/99	W/HM
13	9019196	03/18/99	W/ FEMALE
14	9016406	03/08/99	OUT WITH B/M
15	9006193	01/27/99	B/M SUBJ 99-01586
16	8090545	12/31/98	1045-DEAD ANIMAL
17	8088927	12/24/98	SUBJ INSIDE VEHC
18	8051628	07/30/98	TRAFFIC STOP
19	8027148	04/21/98	FLAGGED DOWN
20	8014404	02/25/98	WITH SUBJECTS
21	8013224	02/20/98	TRAFFIC STOP

PRIOR INCIDENTS AT PRIMARY ADDRESS

1	076519	11/11/99	OUT WITH W/M
2	9073605	10/29/99	Apt3 THEL-THEFT-LAPSED 99-20054
3	9072027	10/22/99	OS-ON SCENE

4	9071823	10/21/99	OS-ON SCENE
5	9069819	10/12/99	1015 -DISTURBANCE
6	9069810	10/11/99	1015-DISTURBANCE 99-18886
7	9069292	10/09/99	ON FOOT
8	9068501	10/06/99	OS-ON SCENE
9	9068266	10/05/99	WITH SUBJ 99-18431
10	9067667	10/02/99	OUT WITH VEHICLE 99-18252
11	9066621	09/28/99	OS-ON SCENE
12	9065996	09/25/99	WANP-WANTED PERSON
13	9062016	09/09/99	OS-ON SCENE
14	9060609	09/03/99	AptOS OS-ON SCENE
15	9058688	08/26/99	Apt7 INV- INVESTIGATION
16	9052948	08/01/99	OS-ON SCENE
17	9047051	07/07/99	AptN OS-ON SCENE
18	9045038	06/28/99	OS-ON SCENE
19	9030518	05/04/99	W/VEH

PRIOR INCIDENTS AT '500 Block

1	9076036	11/08/99	OUT WITH SUBJ
2	9075999	11/08/99	TRAFFIC STOP
3	9072118	10/23/99	TRAFFIC STOP
4	9072059	10/22/99	TRAFFIC STOP 99-19588
5	9070438	10/15/99	TRAFFIC STOP
6	9070439	10/15/99	DIR-DIRECTIONS
7	9066029	09/25/99	TRAFFIC STOP 99-17790
8	9060758	09/03/99	CC - COMMUNITY CONTACT
9	9060319	09/02/99	FP-FREQUENT PATROL
10	9058851	08/26/99	OUT W/FEMALE
11	9058700	08/26/99	FP-FREQUENT PATROL 99-15498
12	9054573	08/08/99	TRAFFIC STOP
13	9053700	08/04/99	TRAFFIC STOP
14	9031666	05/08/99	TRAFFIC STOP 99-08191
15	9031573	05/07/99	FLAG- FLAGGED DOWN
16	9028782	04/26/99	TRAFFIC STOP
17	9018490	03/16/99	TRAFFIC STOP 98-17898
18	9015419	03/03/99	TRAFFIC STOP
19	9014406	02/27/99	DRUG-DRUGS, SELLING,USING,
20	9013749	02/25/99	OS-ON SCENE
21	9012632	02/21/99	TRAFFIC STOP
22	9012192	02/20/99	OS-ON SCENE
23	9012186	02/20/99	OS-ON SCENE
24	9008282	02/05/99	TRAFFIC STOP
25	9005251	01/23/99	FP-FREQUENT PATROL

VICTORIA POLICE DEPARTMENT
POP/PROBLEM SOLVING PROGRAM

REQUEST TO OPEN POP FILE

DATE: 11/18/99

ORIGIN: (XX) OFFICER ( ) AREA DC ( ) AREA LT. ( ) AREA SGT

( ) OTHER ____________

OFFICER ASSIGNED: Townsend, Jeff C. #5105

AREA: 100

PROBLEM LOCATION: ____________

PROBLEM DESCRIPTION: Prostitution/Narcotics

WHEN PROBLEM OCCURS: Night time/Sporadic in the day time.

OTHER COMMENTS: Neighbors are complaining but wish to remain anonymous because they are afraid of retaliation to any action taken.

APPROVAL ROUTE:

DEPUTY CHIEF Richard R. Jones #1085

LIEUTENANT J Kagan 1208

SERGEANT ____________

P-25 (02-01-99)

VICTORIA PD "POP" PROGRAM

OFFICERS LOG:

DATE	INFORMATION
11/26/99	IT APPEARS THE PROSTITUTION TRAFFIC HAS MOVED. NO CALLS ON DAY SHIFT, NOTHING REPORTED FROM NIGHTS. IT APPEARS TO BE WORKING.
12/04/99	IT APPEARS NUMEROUS PROSTITUTES/DEALERS ARE STAYING BEHIND [redacted] AND USING [redacted] AS AN ALIBI I.E. WERE VISITING WATLER. [redacted] WILL BE ADVISED OF THE SITUATION. [redacted] B/F 08/07/61 WAS FOUND IN FRONT YARD, ISSUED CITATION #453927, ATT. CRIMINAL TRESPASS.
2/11/99	CONTACTED TWO INDIVIDUALS IN THE DRIVEWAY OF [redacted], [redacted] 06/21/56 AND [redacted] B/M 07/20/70, BOTH STATED THEY WERE VISITING [redacted]. I CONTACTED [redacted] AND ASKED WHO HAD BEEN VISITING HIM LATELY, HE GAVE TWO NAMES WHICH WERE NOT [redacted] OR [redacted]. [redacted] CITED FOR ATT. CRIM. TRESPASS #453936, [redacted] #453935. WHEN I FIRST CONTACTED THEM I OBSERVED SEVERAL SUBJECTS RUNNING FROM BEHIND [redacted]

(PM:ADMIN-POP:LA 09-14-94

"Corruption in Victoria is not the officer taking money for protection or to look the other way when a crime is committed. The corruption that has occurred here is when officers take advantage of their position of power. Officers who have become corrupt will take advantage of officer discounts or use their power to have physical relations with a woman.

"High ethical standards are necessary to rid a police department of corruption. All new officers are videotaped and asked 'Who made you a high ethical person?' The new officers will talk about their personal experiences and how someone helped them through life. The officers take the videotape home with them and are instructed to view it every employment anniversary. The officers should question themselves: Are they the same person today as they were on the videotape? They were hired because of the type of person they were when the tape was made. Has the occupation changed them? Have their ethics been compromised? New officers are required to fill out a card documenting their personal priorities in life. They are to review their priorities annually. The officers also are required to fill out exit cards. Under what conditions would an officer not do something? That is their exit point. See p.137 of this Supplement for a copy of a VPD exit card.

According to Chief Braaten, the ten commandments of law enforcement are as follows:

1. If you can't make things better - don't make them worse
2. Know the priorities in your life - keep them close at hand
3. Prepare yourself with positive self-talk
4. Civility enhances legitimacy and authority
5. Tension barriers are everywhere
6. Honor others - listen with courtesy
7. The greatest gift you give is sincere empathy
8. Always built trust - always
9. Hold tight to your personal power
10. Even the foolish assess the opposition

"I have seen a change in the integrity of society and young people over the years since I started as a police officer. A national tragedy that is not getting enough attention is the tendency for young people to try to lie their way out of trouble, or just lie to obtain more status. Though their years of growing up, young people have lied and society has allowed them to do so with less punishment than when I was young. When confronted with trouble, many young people today will try to lie their way out of punishment rather than accepting responsibility. They have been successful at lying or skirting the truth and this only compounds the problem.

"Young applicants may try to lie to cover up some of their misdeeds of the past. I do not want a person in this department who will not stand up to the strict ethical standards which the community expects of police officers. Integrity in any police department is a cornerstone. In the last six years I have fired four officers for not telling the truth during an internal investigation. One of these officers was a good officer up to that point but he became scared during an internal investigation and tried to lie his way out of it. If he had told the truth, he probably would have been disciplined but not fired.

"Today those who are interested in law enforcement need to consider the career in reference to their long-term goals. Try to find an agency that they are willing to stay with for a long career. Do not just consider the salary or the positive reputation of the department, but consider the community that you will live in. Consider what you will do in the community when you are not at work. You want to work in a community you are willing to grow with. Equate your success with long-term respect you receive in and out of your job. Last, be a proper, fair authority figure in your community so that the youth of that community have someone to look up to."

My Personal Priorities in Life.
Rank each of the following
(add more if you wish)
1st, 2nd, 3rd, 4th, and so on.

Family	____
Friends	____
Health	____
Honor	____
Liberty	____
Religion	____
Respect	____
Security	____
Wealth	____
__________	____
__________	____

EXIT CARD

This Exit Card records my core values and signifies that I'll Exit rather than compromise.

My Core Values

1. ____________________

2. ____________________

3. ____________________

4. ____________________

Signature ____________________

An Interview With
Charles M. Bell, Assistant Warden
Texas Department of Criminal Justice
Skyview/Hodge Unit
Rusk, Texas

Assistant Warden Charles "Charlie" M. Bell has been employed with TDCJ-ID since December 1984. After graduating high school in 1983, he attended Sam Houston State University in Huntsville, Texas. Charlie was the first in his family to ever attend college. He decided to work for the prison system at the age of 19, to help pay his way through college.

Mr. Bell went straight to work as a correctional officer at the Goree Unit (pronounced GorEE). The offender population consisted of mentally ill offenders, general population offenders, and transient offenders being processed into the system. Mr. Bell was assigned to C-Block his first day in a prison. His sergeant gave him a big brass ring with ten large keys and told him, "they unlock the cells over there." The sergeant left Bell on his own without any other correctional officers around. 'That was scary," recalls Warden Bell.

An offender approached the frightened correctional officer and offered to help. He told Mr. Bell what needed to be done and what offenders might cause him trouble. Mr. Bell was very happy that the offender did not lead him wrong. Three hours later, another correctional officer came back to check on him and found everything going all right.

Another incident Mr. Bell had within his first week of employment was when he was supervising offenders showering. One of the offenders refused to get out of the shower. Mr. Bell felt he was going to have his first physical confrontation. But another offender came to Mr. Bell's assistance and got the disobedient offender to cooperate.

Mr. Bell had a goal of being a senior warden by the age of 35. However, he did not try to be promoted while he attended Sam Houston State. Soon after graduation, Mr. Bell was promoted to sergeant at the Goree Unit. Four years later, in September of 1992, he was promoted to lieutenant at the McConnell Unit in Beeville. Mr. Bell was promoted to captain and transferred to the Stevenson Unit at Cuero in April 1994. Mr. Bell was captain for 17 months before being promoted to major at the same unit. In June 1997, Charlie Bell became Assistant Regional Director for Region IV which serves south Texas. Mr. Bell's last promotion was to Assistant Warden at the Skyview/Hedge Unit in August 1998.

Mr. Bell does not consider his climb up the career ladder as accelerated, but admitted that other people might view it as such. Mr Bell believes his success is due to hard work, and a willingness to relocate to other areas in Texas to obtain a promotion. "You have to take the opportunities where ever they may be in Texas."

Mr. Bell says there are fantastic opportunities in the Institutional Division. Mr. Bell says he has been given the opportunity by the agency to be the best he can be and he thoroughly loves his job. Warden

Bell says "the mission of TDCJ-ID is to provide for the public safety, promote positive change in behavior, reintegrate offenders into society, and assist victims of crime."

Charlie Bell has worked in maximum- and medium-security prisons. His first assignment was in a psychiatric unit and he is currently the Assistant Warden at a co-gender psychiatric in-patient unit and a unit that is for mentally retarded male offenders. Warden Bell readily admits the psychiatric units are the most challenging to work in. The psychiatric units can be stressful to the correctional officers because offenders are criminals with psychological impairments. These units house all types of offenders with mental impairments, from the aggressive to the very passive. The classification process assigns like offenders to common areas of the prison in order to prevent a very aggressive offender from being housed with a very submissive offender. The correctional officer plays an important role in this classification process. If a correctional officer observes an offender who does not meet the specific classification he/she will notify supervisors to have the offender reviewed for appropriate housing in another area of the prison. In the event that a life is in danger, the moving of the offender will be expedited.

Officers who work in a psychiatric in-patient unit receive additional training on dealing with mentally handicapped offenders. Officers are trained on how to communicate to psychiatric offenders and to be more patient. Warden Bell explains "The psychiatric offender might not obey an order because he truly does not understand the order."

Warden Bell was asked if minimum-security prisons are country clubs. "Not at all; minimum-security units allow for the least restrictive confinement based upon current and past behavior, along with the offender's criminal history. As with all the units in TDCJ-ID, the better the offender's behavior, the number of privileges increase. But minimum-security prisons in Texas do not have swimming pools, air conditioning, or golf courses. Offenders must work and/or go to school.

"Many people outside of corrections blame the prisons for not doing a better job of rehabilitating offenders. I believe that the expectation for rehabilitation is too high. Often the Institutional Division must begin by habilitating offenders. The vast majority of offenders committed to the Institutional Division have personality disorders, the most common being anti-social personality disorder. Offenders have never been taught how to cope with frustration or accept responsibility for their behavior. The offenders learned of coping behavior in their free world environment. Therefore, the Institutional Division is unfairly expected to change the offender's personality and way of living in a short time that has been developed and learned over the offender's lifetime.

"There are programs in TDCJ-ID for offenders who want to improve. Programs and services along with necessary professional staff and equipment are available for those who want to develop skills to succeed outside the prison walls. Unfortunately, offenders, especially repeat offenders, lack the motivation to change. These unmotivated offenders will participate in programs and accept services only to look good for their parole hearing. The offenders must have the will to change. TDCJ-ID cannot teach offenders how to be motivated to change. TDCJ-ID does continue to be successful in promoting a positive change in behavior through established programs and services, and a professional correctional staff. For a prison system to attempt to rehabilitate all offenders is overextending the capabilities of the agency at a tremendous cost to the taxpayers, especially when the offenders are not motivated to change. TDCJ-ID will always make sure that offenders are placed in programs that will help them to be reintegrated into society.

“There are 19 private prisons in Texas that contract with TDCJ. There are private prisons in Texas that house either out of state offenders or those convicted for misdemeanors. Of the 19 that work with TDCJ, six are private prisons, six are state jail facilities and seven are private parole revocation confinement facilities. The private facilities help TDCJ-ID keep the offender population below capacity and they provide the service at an average cost to Texas at $34.39 per offender, per day. The state’s cost is an average of $38.71 per offender, per day.

“TDCJ-ID has been very instrumental in the yearly reduction of the crime rate in Texas since 1993. Early in the 1990s TDCJ-ID expanded so that offenders can stay behind bars for a longer period of time. This keeps the offenders off the streets and reduces the motivation to recidivate once the offender is released. The motivation to commit crime is reduced in the Texas youth when they see offenders serving a longer portion of their sentence. Today TDCJ-ID is near capacity, but not overcrowded. Along with the expansion of TDCJ-ID came legislation which lengthened the time offenders must serve in prison before being eligible for parole. Awarding good time credits and early release practices were also changed by legislative acts. Offenders are locked up longer and are not quickly released back into society to do their dirty deeds.

“I am very proud of the community service projects that TDCJ-ID participates in. Offenders can give back to society a portion of what they took. Many offenders have only taken all their lives and the community service projects allow them to give something back. Community service performs jobs that would not otherwise get done: painting schools in the summer, cleaning drainage ditches to prevent flooding, and city beautification projects. In Rusk, the Main Street Project used offenders to renew the sidewalks around the courthouse square. TDCJ-ID also participates in Habitat for Humanity and provides assistance to various food banks.”

“I am also proud of the men and women who work for the Institutional Division. I wish that the rest of society would understand the real duties of the correctional officer because once that is realized, the correctional officer would be more appreciated by citizenry.

“Another program that TDCJ-ID operates is Operation Outreach. This program has offenders talk to troubled or at-risk youth. The youth might be as young as nine years old. The youth are brought into the prison and shown what it is like to call a prison home. The offenders tell the youth the difficulties of institutionalization and the problems that put them in prison. The Skyview Unit brought in about 430 youth in 1999 from surrounding counties as part of this program.

“In the 1980s overcrowding of the prisons was a major issue with TDCJ-ID. The overcrowding was addressed by increasing good time credit, and back-dating that credit for time served in a county jail, releasing offenders 90 days before their scheduled release date. TDCJ-ID had to refuse to admit new offenders in some cases and this made county jails overcrowded. TDCJ-ID paid the county jails for housing offenders who were supposed to be in state prison.”

Warden Bell has seen many changes in the Institutional Division since his first days in 1984. Some of the changes were a result of the *Ruiz vs. Estelle* lawsuit. The most pronounced changes were in medical and psychiatric services provided to the offenders. The health care system is managed by the University of Texas Medical Branch and Texas Tech University. "The medical care provided to the offenders today is as good as what I can get in the free world," Warden Bell explained.

"The *Ruiz* lawsuit also brought about an extensive offender classification system; more support staff is available to offenders such as psychologists, therapists, chaplains, and educational programs. Training for correctional officers has vastly improved. Training has improved to the point that the American Correctional Association now accredits the Moreles Training Academy, in Beeville, Texas. Overall the *Ruiz* lawsuit helped TDCJ-ID and all of Texas. The correctional system is more advanced than it has ever been.

"TDCJ-ID controls offender behavior by two primary plans, a sophisticated classification system and a disciplinary system, which is uniform throughout the state. The classification system is based upon the behavior of the offender while in prison. A correctional officer has an insight into the offender's expected behavior when the officer is aware of the offender's classification.

"The disciplinary plan is a progressive system based upon reducing privileges and good time credit earning status. A lot of good old verbal skills and crisis intervention by the correctional officer can go a long way in controlling an offender's behavior. Offenders have emotions and they experience change just like everyone else. The correctional officers learn how to address the emotions of the offenders. This is a type of control technique. The offenders might not want to hear the message, but when the correctional officers take the offender's emotions into consideration, most will respond positively when the message is communicated.

"The correctional officers will take different approaches to calm an offender down. The officers will first try to resolve the problem informally by explaining to the offender what is expected and the consequences of his misbehavior. The correctional officers will communicate differently when working with a group of offenders such as a work squad or in a day room. The officer must strive to always remember the humanity aspect of the job and that 99% of the offenders will do as they are told if the directive is clear and communicated in a professional manner.

"The discipline of offenders is controlled by statewide policy. The correctional officer will always try to deal with the offender on an informal level before enacting the formal disciplinary process. The discipline is based on the offense committed. A less serious offense is being out of place. This involves the offender being in an area that is not authorized for that particular offender, for example being in a cellblock which he is not assigned. The correctional officer may tell the offender to leave, and if he returns, he will have a formal disciplinary charge [a case] filed against him.

"The formal disciplinary charges can be major cases or minor cases. Past behavior of the offender and the likelihood he will repeat the violation are considered when assessing discipline. Discipline may include reprimand, suspension of privileges, cell restriction, extra work duties, property restriction, loss of good time credit, or solitary confinement. The last two punishments are for a major violation of the rules.

"Unlike the movies, wardens in Texas do not have unregulated power and control over a prison unit. The Institutional Division outlines its policies and procedures and it is the warden's responsibility to see that these are carried out at the prison unit level. Wardens are accountable for their actions to other TDCJ administrators and to the citizens of Texas. Wardens have some latitude and discretion within the guidelines, policies, and state law which allows the wardens to manage.

"There is strict enforcement in the Texas system, but the system also does more for the offender than what is required by state and federal laws. When a large group of people with no social skills and little respect for others are brought together, offender behavior management can only be accomplished by strict control and organization.

"TDCJ-ID has a series of checks and balances to make sure an offender is not placed in solitary because he is an offender with problems. The offender is screened and psychologically tested when he/she first enters the prison. Offender needs assessments are conducted and appropriate referrals are made. All prison units have psychological counseling, medical, and chaplain services (which include volunteers from outside the prison who come to talk to the offenders); substance abuse counselors and teachers throughout the educational program are also available to all offenders. The correctional officers will document and call attention to the offenders who have a rapid change in behavior or routine. Experienced officers and supervisors can easily determine if an offender is having trouble coping or is just an offender who is trouble. TDCJ-ID promotes family contact either by writing, telephone calls, or personal visits by relatives or friends. Offenders who are able to maintain family contacts are normally much less disruptive than those that do not."

Warden Bell's description of problem offenders is the foundation of the disciplinary and privilege system in TDCJ-ID. "Disruptive behavior is an excuse. An offender does not need to resort to violence and assaultive behavior if he/she is motivated not to. Offenders have a choice of what type of behavior he/she will exhibit. Assaultive or disruptive behavior is accountable behavior. A problem offender seldom accepts responsibility for his/her behavior. Nor does he/she want to be held accountable for the behavior.

"Offenders will test the will and fortitude of the correctional officer by intentionally violating a minor rule in front of the correctional officer. The offenders want to observe the correctional officer's reaction to the infraction. A common example is the offender will touch the correctional officer seemingly inadvertently. The officer should sternly tell the offender not to do that again.

"Offenders are some of the best psychologists. Offenders are street wise, they can manipulate and pull the wool over people's eyes, and it may take three or four days for them to realize they have been fooled.

"Offenders adapt to institutional life by first searching for their comfort zone. The offender who is in a large group will search out others who have a similar background, just as people who are in the free world do. For example, college freshmen will seek out similar background students to converse with during their first weeks away from home and in a new environment. Offenders are the same except they will seek out persons with similar street experience. Offenders will get into trouble in the institution because of the people they hang around with. Before the offender was placed in prison he/she got into trouble because of the people he/she associated with. Offenders who have higher levels of education will associate with others who have approximately the same level of education."

Warden Bell was asked, “Are convicted child abusers routinely attacked by other offenders while they are incarcerated?” His reply was, “That was probably true 15 or 20 years ago, but definitely not today.”

Warden Bell has never witnessed an execution of a condemned prisoner, but he knows people who regularly do so as part of their duties. "An execution is not an easy thing to watch. It is not easy to watch someone die. Capital punishment is necessary, but watching an execution gives you a sinking feeling. It is difficult to watch while the IV is hooked up and the condemned offender dies. Even when an officer watches several executions as part of his/her duties, it never gets any easier.

“As of November 1999, 34% of the correctional officers and supervisors working for TDCJ-ID were female. Female correctional officers do the same jobs as men, except strip searches will not be cross gender. Women may pat search a male offender, but male correctional officers cannot pat search a female, except in emergencies. Women are able to do their duties as well as, and in certain instances better than male counter parts. Women often have the ability to de-escalate a hostile situation because there is no machismo. Offenders normally do not view women officers to be as much of a threat as men officers, even though women will get involved with using force just as often as men do. Women have the ability to calm the situations before they resort to force.”

Last, Warden Bell encourages criminal justice majors to learn about correctional science. “Talk to correctional officers about the job. A career in corrections has daily challenges. The opportunities in corrections exceed most other criminal justice agencies. The person who works in corrections can take pride in knowing that he/she can supervise and manage the most difficult group of people in all of Texas.

“Police officers arrest the offender, the prosecutor obtains a conviction, but the correctional officer is the person who keeps the offenders confined and must confront those offenders every single day. The correctional officers must protect the community by keeping the worst people off the streets and also protect other officers and staff.

“Many correctional officers are proud of the job that they do, and I am very proud and privileged to work with them.”